CHILLI
& SPICE

**100 RECIPES TO HEAT UP
& SPICE UP YOUR LIFE**

CHILLI
&
SPICE

This edition published by Parragon Books Ltd in 2017
LOVE FOOD is an imprint of Parragon Books Ltd

Parragon Books Ltd
Chartist House
15–17 Trim Street
Bath BA1 1HA, UK
www.parragon.com/lovefood

ISBN 978-1-4748-3808-5

Printed in China

NOTES FOR THE READER

This book uses both metric and imperial measurements. Follow the
same units of measurement throughout; do not mix metric and imperial.
All spoon measurements are level: teaspoons are assumed to be 5 ml,
and tablespoons are assumed to be 15 ml. Unless otherwise stated, milk
is assumed to be full fat, eggs and individual fruits and vegetables are
medium, pepper is freshly ground black pepper and salt is table salt.
A pinch of salt is calculated as $\frac{1}{16}$ of a teaspoon. Unless otherwise stated,
all root vegetables should be peeled prior to using.

The times given are an approximate guide only. Preparation times differ
according to the techniques used by different people and the cooking
times may also vary from those given.

For best results, use a food thermometer when cooking meat.
Check the latest government guidelines for current advice.

Take care when preparing chillies. The fiery heat comes from the chemical
compound capsaicin, located in the white pithy inner core or rib of the
chilli. Capsaicin can aggravate skin and eyes so always wash your hands
thoroughly after handling chillies. If your skin is sensitive, wear plastic
gloves. Never touch your eyes or mouth after handling chillies without
thoroughly washing your hands first with soap and water.

CONTENTS

CHILLIES & SPICES
A CULINARY JOURNEY

If you're tired of preparing the same predictable meals and are craving something with a little more oomph, then look no further. Chilli & Spice features 101 sizzling recipes from around the globe to help jazz up your dishes – warming starters, snacks and sides; fiery vegetarian, meat, and fish mains; and tantalizing sweet treats.

SPICES

In ancient times, spices were used to prevent ingredients from going off and to disguise food with strong odours and unpleasant flavours. As they became popular for their aromatic flavours, spices were integrated into everyday cuisine, with countries and regions developing their own unique signature dishes based on available indigenous spices. Over time, people discovered the remarkable medicinal properties of specific spices.

Nowadays, we may not give much thought to our ubiquitous, affordable spices as we sprinkle them liberally over ingredients, but they have an incredible history. Once the world's biggest and most dominant industry, the spice trade produced great wealth for many nations. Spices were such precious commodities that nutmeg and pepper were worth more than gold.

The spice trade began with camel caravans in the Middle East some 4,000 years ago. Arabic spice traders spun elaborate myths about how hard the spices were to come by, thereby adding to their allure and driving up prices. The Silk Road connecting Asia with North Africa and Europe played a vital role in building mighty civilizations

and empires such as those of China, India, Egypt, Persia, Arabia and Rome.

For centuries, Middle-Eastern and North African traders monopolized the spice trade, becoming increasingly wealthy and powerful, and forcing European merchants to pay excessively high prices. By the 1400s, even the nobility was struggling to pay for aromatic luxuries, so explorers were dispatched overseas in search of alternative trade routes.

First to cross the Atlantic Ocean was Italian explorer Christopher Columbus, who accidentally stumbled across the Americas in 1492 while looking for precious black pepper and a more direct route to India. He discovered new fruit and vegetables, including maize, potatoes, pumpkins, pineapple, avocados and papayas, and perhaps most notably the much-loved chilli pepper.

In 1497, Portuguese explorer Vasco de Gama became the first to sail directly from Africa to India. His sea route around Africa opened up trade between Europe and Asia and led to a Portuguese dominance of the spice trade that endured for centuries.

As spice cultivation began to spread around the world, availability became more widespread, and prices fell. Highly valuable spices, such as pepper, cinnamon and nutmeg, are no longer the precious products they once were, but they are just as popular today, still cherished for their vibrant colours, pungent flavours and enticing aromas.

CHILLIES

Chilli peppers are the fruit pods of perennial, woody-stemmed shrubs that belong to the *Capsicum* genus They originate from Central America where archeologists have found traces of their consumption by humans dating back to 7500 BCE. Chillies have been used as a primary ingredient in Mexican cooking for hundreds of years.

Although chilli peppers were unheard of in Europe until Columbus's 15th-century discovery, they had already played a major part in Asian cuisine for some 2,000 years. With the increase in shipping during the 16th and 17th centuries, Indian and Chinese flavourings spread around the globe. Chillies soon became a favourite way to add piquancy to cooking, especially as they were much cheaper than pepper.

Chillies have never fallen out of favour, and today around 25 per cent of the world's population enjoy them in their daily diet. There is a huge variety to choose from, including bird's eye, Scotch bonnet, habañero and jalapeño. They are grown widely in many parts of the world as an important commercial crop, but India is the biggest cultivator, exporter and consumer of this hot pod.

As well as their fiery flavours, chillies also have many nutritional and health-boosting benefits. The pod's heat-emitting chemical compound, capsaicin, has anti-bacterial, anti-carcinogenic, and pain-relieving properties, and may also lower bad cholesterol. Fresh red and green chillies are a rich source of vitamins A, B and C, as well as minerals such as iron, potassium, magnesium and copper.

Chillies can be bought fresh, dried or powdered. Fresh varieties come in vibrant colours of red, green, orange and yellow, and you should look for firm, plump ones with healthy stalks. Avoid buying chillies that are soft, discoloured, missing their caps or have spots or signs of mould. Store them in the fridge or a cool, dark place for up to two weeks, then wash before use. The most flavoursome dried chilli peppers are the sun-dried variety. Look for ones with smooth, unblemished skins with a slight bendiness to them. Use within a year.

SPICES IN COOKING

Spices comprise all the dried parts, except the leaves, of a tropical plant or tree, such as the seeds, bark, roots, and berries. Popular spices, which are used to enrich the flavours of culinary ingredients, include mustard, pepper, paprika, cloves, caraway seeds, cinnamon, ginger and nutmeg, to name just a few of them.

As well as their appealing aromatic properties, many spices are renowned for their healing attributes. For example, turmeric is thought to be an excellent anti-inflammatory. Cloves aid digestion and have anti-bacterial properties, while ginger helps stave off nausea.

Spices may be dry fried in a hot wok or pan or ground first with a pestle and mortar, then mixed into a paste with a little water. Once spices are ground their flavour does begin to deteriorate, so

it's preferable if you can grind your own – using a mortar and pestle or coffee grinder – immediately before cooking for optimum flavour. If this is not possible, store bought ground spices in a cool place and use within six months of purchase.

CHILLI PREPARATION

To decide whether a chilli is mild or hot, first examine its shape. Milder chillies tend to have broader shoulders and blunter tips, whereas hotter ones have narrower shoulders and more pointy tips. Chillies of the same variety can vary in heat intensity. To test before adding to your recipe, try halving the chilli and hold it just under your nose. If you feel a buzz, then you know it's a hot one!

Take care when preparing chillies. The fiery heat comes from the chemical compound capsaicin, which is located in the white pithy inner core or rib of the chilli. Contrary to popular belief, the seeds don't actually contain any heat, but, because they lie close to the pith, they may acquire a layer of the hot compound. Capsaicin can aggravate skin and eyes so it is important to wash hands thoroughly after handling. If you want to reduce the intensity of a chilli's heat then remove the pith and seeds. If it is still too hot to handle, then you can try stirring in some yogurt, sour cream or ghee to help take it down a notch.

We hope you enjoy your chilli and spice journey, on the pages that follow. You will find an impressive range of recipes with the characteristic tastes and flavours of many different types of chilli and spice, from the spices star anise and nutmeg to jalapeño and Scotch bonnet chillies.

APPETIZERS & SNACKS

Prepare to tantalize your taste buds with this enticing selection of piquant hors d'oeuvres and nibbles. The mouth-watering flavours include hot Tabbouleh-Stuffed Jalapeños, Griddled Harissa Prawn Skewers, Little Curried Crab Cakes, Ultimate Nachos with Beef, protein-packed Spice-Roasted Edamame & Cranberries and the finger-lickingly moreish Five-Spice Cashews.

TABBOULEH-STUFFED
JALAPEÑOS

MAKES: 48	PREP TIME: 22 mins	COOK TIME: 10–12 mins

JALAPEÑO PEPPERS ARE SMALL IN SIZE BUT CAN PACK A PUNCH WITH FLAVOUR AND NUTRITION. PART OF THE NIGHTSHADE FAMILY, THESE LITTLE PEPPERS DERIVE THEIR HEAT FROM A NATURAL COMPOUND CALLED CAPSAICIN, KNOWN TO OFFER POWERFUL HEALTH BENEFITS.

INGREDIENTS

70 g/2½ oz quinoa
100 g/3½ oz fresh parsley, chopped
100 g/3½ oz fresh mint, chopped
100 g/3½ oz fresh coriander, chopped
1 preserved lemon, chopped
1 tbsp walnuts, chopped
seeds from 1 pomegranate
24 jalapeño chillies, halved and deseeded
2 avocados, peeled, stoned and sliced
juice of 1 lemon
salt and pepper (optional)

1. To make tabbouleh, cook the quinoa according to the packet instructions. Drain and refresh under cold water, then drain again. Place in a large bowl.

2. Add the parsley, mint, coriander, preserved lemon, walnuts and pomegranate seeds and mix thoroughly. Season to taste with salt and pepper, if using.

3. Spoon the tabbouleh into the jalapeños. Top each one with a couple of slices of avocado, then squeeze over the lemon juice to serve.

VARIATION
FOR A DIFFERENT TOPPING, TRY A TABLESPOON OF HUMMUS SPRINKLED WITH TOASTED SUNFLOWER SEEDS AND SMOKED PAPRIKA.

VEGETABLE SAMOSAS

MAKES: 14	PREP TIME: 40–45 mins, plus resting	COOK TIME: 1 hr

IT TAKES A LITTLE PRACTICE TO MASTER SHAPING THESE PASTRIES. MAKE SURE YOU SIMMER THE FILLING MIXTURE UNTIL IT IS QUITE DRY BEFORE USING.

INGREDIENTS

250 g/9 oz plain flour

½ tsp salt

40 g/1½ oz ghee or butter

½ tbsp lemon juice

100–125 ml/3½–4 fl oz cold water

10 g/¼ oz ghee or butter, for greasing

vegetable or groundnut oil, for deep-frying

FILLING

55 g/2 oz ghee or 4 tbsp vegetable or groundnut oil

1 onion, very finely chopped

2 garlic cloves, crushed

1 potato, very finely diced

2 carrots, very finely chopped

2 tsp mild, medium or hot curry powder, to taste

1½ tsp ground coriander

1 tsp ground turmeric

1 fresh green chilli, deseeded and finely chopped

1 tsp salt

½ tsp black mustard seeds

300 ml/10 fl oz cold water

100 g/3½ oz frozen peas

55 g/2 oz cauliflower florets, finely chopped

1. To make the filling, melt the ghee in a large frying pan over a medium–high heat. Add the onion and garlic and fry for 5–8 minutes, until soft. Stir in the potato and carrots and fry for 5 minutes. Stir in the spices, chilli, salt and mustard seeds. Pour in the water and bring to the boil. Reduce the heat to very low and simmer, uncovered, for about 15 minutes. Add the peas and cauliflower and simmer until the vegetables are tender and the liquid has evaporated. Remove from the heat and set aside.

2. Meanwhile, sift the flour and salt into a bowl. Make a well, add the ghee and lemon juice and work them into the flour. Gradually add the water until the mixture comes together to form a soft dough and knead for about 10 minutes, until smooth. Shape into a ball, cover with a damp tea towel and leave to rest for 15 minutes.

3. Divide the dough into seven pieces. On a lightly greased work surface, roll each piece of dough into a 20-cm/8-inch round, then cut in half to make two semi-circles. Keep the remaining pieces of dough covered.

4. Working with one semi-circle at a time, wet the edges with water. Place 2 teaspoons of filling on the dough, just off-centre. Fold one side into the centre, covering the filling. Fold the other side in the opposite direction, overlapping the first fold to form a cone shape. Wet the open edge with water and press to seal.

5. Heat the oil for deep-frying in a saucepan or deep-fryer until it reaches 180–190°C/350–375°F. Working in batches, deep-fry the samosas for 2–3 minutes, flipping them over once, until golden brown. Remove with a slotted spoon and drain well on kitchen paper. Serve warm or at room temperature.

SPICY ONION FRITTERS

SERVES: 4	PREP TIME: 10–15 mins	COOK TIME: 25–30 mins

THESE SERIOUSLY TASTY SPICED ONION FRITTERS ARE EXTREMELY DIFFICULT TO RESIST! THEY ARE A POPULAR STREET SNACK ALL OVER INDIA AND ARE BEST ENJOYED WITH CHUTNEY FOR DIPPING.

INGREDIENTS

150 g/5½ oz gram flour

1 tsp salt, or to taste

small pinch of bicarbonate of soda

25 g/1 oz ground rice

1 tsp fennel seeds

1 tsp cumin seeds

2 fresh green chillies, finely chopped (deseeded if you like)

2 large onions (about 400 g/ 14 oz), sliced into half-rings and separated

15 g/½ oz fresh coriander, leaves and stalks, finely chopped

200 ml/7 fl oz cold water

vegetable or groundnut oil, for deep-frying

1. Sift the gram flour into a large bowl and add the salt, bicarbonate of soda, ground rice, fennel seeds and cumin seeds. Mix together well, then add the chillies, onions and coriander. Gradually pour in the water and mix until a thick batter is formed and the onions are thoroughly coated with it.

2. Heat enough oil for deep-frying in a large saucepan or deep-fryer to 180–190°C/350–375°F, or until a cube of bread browns in 30 seconds. Add as many small amounts (each about ½ tablespoon) of the batter as will fit in a single layer, without overcrowding the pan. Reduce the heat slightly and cook the fritters for 8–10 minutes, until golden brown and crisp.

3. Use a slotted spoon to remove the fritters from the oil and drain well on kitchen paper. Continue frying until all the batter mixture has been used. Serve hot.

GRIDDLED HARISSA PRAWN SKEWERS

| SERVES: 4 | PREP TIME: 20 mins, plus 30 mins marinating | COOK TIME: 4–6 mins |

THESE FIERY TUNISIAN-INSPIRED PRAWN SKEWERS ARE GREAT AS PART OF A MEZE FEAST OR AS A STARTER. YOU WILL NEED FOUR WOODEN SKEWERS.

INGREDIENTS

250 g/9 oz raw king prawns, peeled and deveined, thawed if frozen

2 tsp rose harissa

1 tsp fine sea salt

2 garlic cloves, finely chopped

4 tbsp finely chopped fresh coriander

2 tbsp olive oil

pinch of sea salt flakes

1 lemon, cut into wedges, to serve

1. Mix the prawns, rose harissa, fine sea salt, garlic and half the coriander together in a large bowl. Cover and marinate in the refrigerator for 30 minutes.

2. Soak four wooden skewers in water for 20 minutes, then drain well. Thread the prawns onto the skewers and brush them lightly with the oil.

3. Heat a griddle pan or heavy-based frying pan over a high heat until smoking hot. Lay the skewers on the pan, reduce the heat slightly and cook for 4–6 minutes, or until pink and cooked through, turning halfway.

4. Serve the skewers immediately, scattered with the remaining coriander and the sea salt flakes, with lemon wedges for squeezing over.

LITTLE CURRIED CRAB CAKES WITH AVOCADO SALAD

MAKES: 8	PREP TIME: 20 mins	COOK TIME: 8 mins

ONCE YOU'VE DONE THE PREPARATION, THESE LITTLE CRAB CAKES ARE EASY TO PUT TOGETHER, AND ARE PERFECTLY COMPLEMENTED BY THE TANGY, CHILLI-INFUSED AVOCADO SALAD.

INGREDIENTS

300 g/10½ oz white crabmeat

150 g/5½ oz canned drained sweetcorn kernels

100 g/3½ oz wholemeal panko breadcrumbs

1 large egg, beaten

1½ tbsp light mayonnaise

1½ tbsp fat-free Greek-style yogurt

2 tbsp snipped fresh chives

2 tsp Dijon mustard

1 tsp curry powder

¼ tsp pepper

10 sprays cooking spray, for oiling

SALAD

1 large ripe avocado

1 tomato, finely chopped

juice of ½ lime

small bunch of fresh coriander, leaves only

½ fresh red jalapeño chilli, deseeded and finely chopped

3 spring onions, chopped

1. Mix the crabmeat, sweetcorn, breadcrumbs, egg, mayonnaise, yogurt, chives, mustard, curry powder and pepper together in a bowl.

2. Using your hands, shape the mixture into eight patties. Spray a non-stick frying pan with cooking spray to coat, then heat to just below medium-hot and add the patties to the pan. Cook the patties for 4 minutes, without turning or moving them.

3. Meanwhile, make the salad. Stone, peel and slice the avocado, then lightly crush it in a bowl. Add the tomato, lime juice, coriander leaves, chilli and spring onions, and stir to combine.

4. Spray the tops of the patties with more cooking spray, then use a metal spatula to turn each one over carefully. Cook for a further 3 minutes, or until the crab cakes are golden and piping hot. Serve immediately, topped with the avocado salad.

CHILLI PEPPERS & THE SCOVILLE SCALE

Chilli peppers are a small variety of Capsicum, a genus of tropical pepper plants distinctive for their heat. Ranging from green and yellow to orange, red and black, there are more than 200 varieties.

The oil that creates the heat in chillies is called *capsaicin*. The amount of this oil in individual chillies can vary dramatically even within the same chilli type. The piquancy or hotness of chilli peppers is measured using the Scoville Scale, with units measured as SHU. This scale measures how much *capsaicin* is present in a chilli. So a sweet pepper scores 0, and a pimento scores 100–1,000, moving right up to the Carolina Reaper at 1,500,000–2,200,000 SHU.

The chillies shown within these pages include the following varieties:

Anaheim peppers are a milder variety of the New Mexico chilli pepper. They have a lime-green pod in a long, slender shape and have a mild, sweet, peppery flavour. They measure 500–2,500 SHU.

New Mexico Chillies are green chillis with a flavour that has been likened to an onion, with a subtle hint of sweetness and spiciness. They measure between 800–1,400 SHU on the heat scale.

Cherry Bomb chillies are small, round, and cherry-shaped. They have a pleasant sweetness and are 2,500–5,000 SHU.

Guajillo chillies, a dried form of the mirasol chilli, have a refreshing sweet quality and a tart, fruity flavour and are 2,500–5,000 SHU.

Jalapeño chillies can be used fresh or pickled and can range from moderate to fiery heat, or 2,500–5,000 SHU on the Scoville scale. These chillies are dried and smoked to make chipotles which have a deep, sweet flavour.

Serrano chillies have a substantial heat kick, rating between 8,000 and 23,000 SHU. They are easy to use in salsas as they don't need steaming or peeling before use.

Tabasco chillies are small and hot and have a unique, smoky flavour that is the main contributor to the distinctive taste of Tabasco sauce. They measure 30,000–50,000 SHU.

Bird's eye chillies are small and powerful chillis, measuring 50,000–100,000 SHU – they have a spicy, fruity taste and are often used in South-east Asian cooking.

Habañero chillies have a subtle fruity flavour and measure 100,000–350,000 SHU, so avoid these unless you relish a meal that is blow-your-head-off hot.

Scotch Bonnet chillies, also known as Caribbean red peppers, are lantern-shaped red-hot chillies which can be yellow, green or red. They have a sweeter flavour than habañero and a powerful heat rating of 100,000–350,000 SHU.

Carolina Reaper is currently the world's hottest pepper measuring 1,500,000–2,200,000 SHU. The chilli has a scorpion's tail and a sweet, fruity flavour before the heat hits.

CHIPOTLE TURKEY
CROQUETTES

MAKES: 16	PREP TIME: 35–40 mins	COOK TIME: 20–25 mins

THESE SUPER-HOT CROQUETTES ARE BAKED RATHER THAN FRIED AND THE LEAN TURKEY IS PACKED WITH HEALTHY MINERALS SUCH AS IRON, ZINC, POTASSIUM AND PHOSPHORUS.

INGREDIENTS

1–2 tbsp olive oil

4 spring onions, quartered

1 small red pepper, deseeded and cut into chunks

1 carrot, coarsely grated

2 tsp fresh thyme leaves

500 g/1 lb 2 oz fresh turkey breast mince

1 fresh Carolina Reaper chilli, very finely chopped

1 small dried chipotle chilli, finely chopped

1 egg

1 tbsp cold water

25 g/1 oz freshly grated Parmesan cheese

55 g/2 oz golden linseeds, finely ground

sea salt and pepper (optional)

AVOCADO DIP

1 large ripe avocado, halved and stoned

grated zest and juice of 1 lime

2 tbsp fat-free Greek-style yogurt

1. Preheat the oven to 200°C/400°F/Gas Mark 6. Brush a baking sheet with a little of the oil and line with baking paper. Finely chop the onions and red pepper in a food processor. Add the carrot, thyme and turkey, then sprinkle over the fresh and dried chillies and a little salt and pepper, if using. Process until evenly mixed.

2. Scoop out dessertspoons of the mixture onto a chopping board to make 16 oval-shaped mounds, then press them into neater shapes between your hands.

3. Lightly mix the egg, water and a little salt and pepper together in a shallow dish. Mix the cheese and linseeds in a separate shallow dish. Dip the croquettes, one at a time, into the egg, lift out with two forks, draining well, then roll in the cheese mixture. Place on the prepared baking sheet. Continue until all the croquettes are well coated.

4. Bake in the preheated oven for 20–25 minutes, until golden, turning halfway through cooking and brushing with the remaining oil, if needed. To check that they are cooked, cut one croquette in half – the juices will run clear with no traces of pink.

5. When the croquettes are almost ready to serve, make the dip. Scoop the avocado from the shell, mash with the lime juice and zest, and mix with the yogurt. Spoon into a small bowl set on a large plate, then arrange the hot croquettes around the dish and serve immediately.

STICKY TURKEY KEBABS

SERVES: 2	PREP TIME: 20 mins, plus chilling	COOK TIME: 1 hr 30 mins

THE SOUTH WEST OF TURKEY IS WELL KNOWN FOR ITS SPICY KEBABS. HERE GARLIC, GINGER AND SOY COMBINE WITH THE PAPRIKA AND CUMIN IN THE SPICY RUB TO GIVE THESE KEBABS A GENTLE KICK.

INGREDIENTS

280 g/10 oz turkey breast meat, cubed

360 g/12½ oz cooked long-grain rice, to serve

salad leaves, to garnish

SPICE RUB
1 tbsp soft dark brown sugar

¼ tsp paprika

¼ tsp ground cumin

¼ tsp salt

¼ tsp pepper

STICKY SAUCE
1 tbsp vegetable oil

1 onion, finely chopped

2 garlic cloves, finely chopped

2.5-cm/1-inch piece ginger, grated

3 tbsp tomato ketchup

3 tbsp white wine or cider vinegar

3 tbsp soy sauce

2 tbsp soft light brown sugar

200 ml/7 fl oz water

1. Put the turkey into a bowl and add the spice rub ingredients, mixing well to coat. Chill in the refrigerator for at least 1 hour.

2. Meanwhile, make the sauce. Heat the oil in a saucepan over a medium heat, add the onion, garlic and ginger and cook for 5 minutes. Add the ketchup, wine vinegar, soy sauce, sugar and water and bring to the boil. Reduce the heat and simmer for 1 hour, stirring regularly, until the mixture is thick and sticky.

3. If using wooden skewers, soak them in water for 30 minutes to prevent them from burning. Preheat the barbecue or grill to hot. Thread the turkey pieces onto the skewers and lay them on a sheet of foil. Set aside some of the sticky sauce for serving, then brush a little of the sticky sauce on the kebabs. Cook the kebabs under the preheated barbecue or grill for 10–15 minutes, turning and brushing with more of the sticky sauce until cooked. Serve with the rice and any remaining sticky sauce, garnished with salad leaves.

STICKY BOURBON
CHICKEN WINGS

SERVES: 4	PREP TIME: 20 mins	COOK TIME: 20–30 mins

PAPRIKA IS THE KEY SPICE PLAYER HERE, BUT IT HAS THE HELP OF ITS FRIENDS GROUND CUMIN, WORCESTERSHIRE SAUCE, CHIPOTLE PASTE AND, LAST BUT NOT LEAST, BOURBON. REPLACE THE BOURBON WITH APPLE JUICE IF YOU PREFER.

INGREDIENTS

1 kg/2 lb 4 oz chicken wings, tips removed
1 tbsp vegetable oil, for brushing

RUB
1 tbsp paprika
½ tsp ground cumin
1 tsp dried thyme
1 tsp dried oregano
1 tsp salt
1 tsp pepper

BOURBON GLAZE
2 tbsp bourbon
2 tbsp cider vinegar
1 tbsp Worcestershire sauce
2 tbsp black treacle
2 tbsp tomato ketchup
2 tbsp chipotle paste
1 tbsp American-style mustard
½ tsp salt
½ tsp pepper

1. To make the rub, combine all the ingredients in a large bowl.

2. Cut each chicken wing in half. Add the wing pieces to the bowl containing the rub and turn until coated thoroughly.

3. To make the bourbon glaze, place a medium-sized saucepan over a medium heat. Add the bourbon and flambé. When the flames have gone, add the remaining glaze ingredients and simmer over a medium heat until the sauce has reduced by half.

4. Prepare the barbecue for direct cooking and preheat to medium-hot.

5. Thread half of the chicken wing pieces onto two metal skewers, creating a raft shape. Repeat with the remaining wings. Brush the wings with the bourbon glaze.

6. Lightly brush the barbecue rack with the oil and cook the wings for 10 minutes on each side, brushing with more glaze as they cook.

7. Cook until the chicken is tender and the juices run clear when a skewer is inserted into the thickest part of the meat. The meat should come away easily from the bone. Remove from the skewers and serve.

MASALA PRAWN CAKES

MAKES: 20	PREP TIME: 20 mins, plus chilling	COOK TIME: 12–15 minutes

PERFECT AS CANAPÉS, THESE PRAWN CAKES ARE PACKED WITH THE PUNCHY, FRESH FLAVOURS OF GARLIC, GINGER, COCONUT, CHILLI, CORIANDER AND MINT. SQUEEZE OVER A LITTLE FRESH LIME JUICE AND SERVE WITH A CHILLED DRINK.

INGREDIENTS

800 g/1 lb 12 oz raw tiger prawns, peeled and deveined

2 fresh red chillies, deseeded and very finely chopped

6 tbsp finely chopped fresh coriander

6 tbsp finely chopped fresh mint

1 tsp coconut cream

4 spring onions, finely sliced

2 garlic cloves, finely chopped

2 tsp finely grated fresh ginger

8 tbsp fresh white breadcrumbs

2 tsp ground cumin

1 tsp chilli powder

1 small egg, lightly beaten

4 tbsp vegetable or groundnut oil

lime wedges, to serve

1. Roughly chop the prawns and place them in a food processor with the remaining ingredients, apart from the oil. Blend to a coarse paste. Transfer the mixture to a bowl, cover and chill in the refrigerator for at least 6–8 hours, or overnight.

2. Preheat the oven to 200°C/400°F/Gas Mark 6. Line a baking tray with baking paper.

3. Shape the fish mixture into 20 small patties, approximately 4 cm/1½ inches in diameter. Place on the prepared baking tray and lightly brush with the oil. Bake in the preheated oven for 12–15 minutes, or until slightly puffed up and light golden.

4. Serve warm or at room temperature with lime wedges for squeezing over.

ULTIMATE NACHOS
WITH BEEF

SERVES: 2	PREP TIME: 10 mins	COOK TIME: 30 mins

WHEN YOU'RE EXPECTING CHILLI LOVERS FOR DINNER, THIS IS A REALLY QUICK AND EASY DISH TO SERVE. THE SAUCE IS SPICY HOT, SO WILL KEEP YOUR TONGUE FIRED UP, AND ANY LEFTOVERS MAKE A DELICIOUS TACO FILLING.

INGREDIENTS

2 tbsp olive oil

1 onion, chopped

200 g/7 oz fresh beef mince

1 tbsp dried oregano

1 tbsp paprika

1 tbsp ground cumin

400 g/14 oz passata

225 ml/8 fl oz water

30 g/1 oz butter

30 g/1 oz plain flour

450 ml/15 fl oz milk, warmed

100 g/3½ oz Cheddar cheese, grated

100 g/3½ oz Monterey Jack cheese, grated

1 tbsp American mustard

55 g/2 oz Parmesan cheese, grated

200 g/7 oz tortilla chips

1 ripe avocado

100 g/3½ oz pickled jalapeños, drained

1 small red onion, finely chopped

salt and pepper (optional)

1. In a medium-sized pan, heat the oil over a medium–high heat and add the onion. Cook for 5 minutes, or until translucent and slightly golden. Add the mince and cook for a further 5 minutes, breaking up the meat with a wooden spoon until it starts to brown.

2. Add the oregano, paprika, cumin, passata and water, and cook over a low heat for 20 minutes, or until reduced by half. Season to taste with salt and pepper, if using, and set aside, keeping warm.

3. Meanwhile, melt the butter in a medium-sized pan, add the flour and mix well with a wooden spoon. Slowly add the warm milk, trying to avoid any lumps from forming, until the sauce thickens and starts to boil. Turn off the heat and add the Cheddar cheese, Monterey Jack cheese, American mustard and half the Parmesan cheese. Stir until smooth, season to taste with salt and pepper, if using, and set aside.

4. On a large serving platter, ladle over half of the mince. Place tortilla chips on top, followed by the rest of the mince, then top with the cheese sauce.

5. Cut the avocado in half, remove the stone, peel and chop into small pieces. Scatter the avocado pieces over the nachos along with the jalapeños, chopped red onion and the remaining Parmesan cheese. Serve immediately.

SPICY OVEN-BAKED SCOTCH EGGS

SERVES: 4	PREP TIME: 25 mins	COOK TIME: 30 mins

THESE SCOTCH EGGS ARE PACKED WITH FLAVOUR, BUT ARE LOWER IN FAT AND SIMPLER TO PREPARE THAN THE ORIGINAL PICNIC FARE INVENTED BY LONDON DEPARTMENT STORE FORTNUM AND MASON.

INGREDIENTS

4 large eggs

1 tbsp oil, for oiling

300 g/10½ oz sausages, skins removed

1 tbsp mild curry paste

1 tsp onion seeds

2 tbsp fresh flat-leaf parsley leaves, roughly chopped

55 g/2 oz fresh white breadcrumbs

2 tbsp milk

chutney, to serve

1. Place the eggs in a saucepan and cover with cold water. Bring to the boil, then remove from the heat. Cover the pan and leave to stand for 6 minutes. Drain and cool under cold running water, then carefully peel off the shells.

2. Preheat the oven to 190°C/375°F/Gas Mark 5. Lightly oil a baking tray or line with non-stick baking paper. Place the sausage meat, curry paste, onion seeds and parsley in a bowl. Mix well. Add the breadcrumbs and milk and mix again. Divide into four equal portions.

3. Lay a piece of clingfilm on the work surface. Place a quarter of the sausage mixture on top and flatten with clean hands to a diameter of about 13 cm/5 inches. Place an egg in the centre and use the clingfilm to lift and mould the mixture around it. Smooth over the edges to seal. Place on the baking tray. Repeat with the remaining sausage mixture and eggs.

4. Bake in the preheated oven for 25 minutes until lightly browned, and serve with chutney.

SPICE-ROASTED EDAMAME & CRANBERRIES

SERVES: 4	PREP TIME: 15 mins	COOK TIME: 15 mins

FROZEN EDAMAME OR YOUNG SOYA BEANS MAKE A HEALTHY, PROTEIN-PACKED SNACK AND THEIR HIGH LEVELS OF FIBRE KEEP YOU FEELING FULLER LONGER.

INGREDIENTS

350 g/12 oz frozen edamame (soya) beans

5-cm/2-inch piece fresh ginger, peeled and finely grated

1 tsp Szechuan peppercorns, roughly crushed

1 tbsp soy sauce

1 tbsp olive oil

3 small star anise

40 g/1½ oz dried cranberries

1. Preheat the oven to 180°C/350°F/Gas Mark 4. Place the beans in a roasting tin, then sprinkle over the ginger and peppercorns, drizzle with soy sauce and oil, and mix together.

2. Tuck the star anise in among the beans, then roast, uncovered, in the preheated oven for 15 minutes.

3. Stir in the cranberries and leave to cool. Spoon into a small jar and eat within 12 hours.

TIP

EDAMAME BEANS ARE EXTREMELY VERSATILE AND PACK A MUCH GREATER NUTRITIONAL PUNCH THAN FROZEN PEAS.

FIVE-SPICE
CASHEWS

SERVES: 8	PREP TIME: 5 mins	COOK TIME: 10–12 mins

PEPPERCORNS, STAR ANISE, FENNEL, CLOVES AND CINNAMON COMBINE HERE WITH THE NATURAL SWEETNESS OF CASHEWS. THIS NUTTY CONCOCTION PERFORMS AT EVERY LEVEL, WHETHER FOR A SNACK OR AN APPETIZER.

INGREDIENTS

1 tbsp groundnut oil, for oiling

½ tsp Szechuan peppercorns

2 star anise

½ tsp fennel seeds

6 whole cloves

½ tsp ground cinnamon

2 tbsp water

50 g/1¾ oz soft light brown sugar

1 tsp salt

250 g/9 oz unsalted, toasted cashew nuts

1. Preheat the oven to 200°C/400°F/Gas Mark 6. Lightly oil a baking tray and a large piece of foil.

2. In a spice grinder, grind together the peppercorns, star anise pods, fennel seeds and cloves until finely ground. Add the cinnamon and mix well.

3. Put the water and sugar into a medium-sized saucepan and heat over a medium heat, stirring constantly, for 2 minutes, or until the sugar has dissolved. Add the spice mixture and salt and stir to mix well. Add the nuts and stir to coat completely. Cook, stirring, for a further minute.

4. Transfer the nuts to the prepared tin and spread out in an even layer. Roast in the preheated oven for 6–8 minutes until most of the liquid has evaporated. Transfer the nuts to the prepared foil and separate them so that they don't stick together. Leave to cool completely before serving.

5. Store in an airtight container at room temperature for up to 2 weeks.

LIGHT MEALS & FAST FARE

Looking for a light lunch or supper? Or a speedy, satisfying solution when you're short of time? Then this warming range of flavoursome recipes should hit the spot. From hearty soups and fresh salads to spicy omelettes and tacos, each dish promises to satisfy your appetite. How about Vegetable Noodle Broth, Chilli Squid with Watercress or a Fiery Fish Finger Sandwich?

CHICKEN SOUP
WITH CHILLI & COUSCOUS

SERVES: 4	PREP TIME: 20 mins	COOK TIME: 1¾ hours

THE BROTH FOR THIS CLASSIC MIDDLE EASTERN SOUP IS MADE WITH A WHOLE CHICKEN, WHICH IS THEN TORN INTO STRIPS BEFORE BEING ADDED BACK TO THE SOUP. LEBANESE SEVEN SPICE IS A MIXTURE OFTEN USED IN DISHES WITH MINCED BEEF OR LAMB, AS WELL AS POULTRY.

INGREDIENTS

1 tbsp olive oil

2 onions, finely chopped

1 red chilli, deseeded and finely chopped

1 tsp ground cumin

1 tsp paprika

1 tsp granulated sugar

2 tsp dried mint

1 tbsp tomato purée

100 g/3½ oz couscous

3 tbsp finely chopped fresh coriander, to garnish

1 lemon, cut into wedges, to serve

STOCK

1 ready-to-cook chicken, weighing 1.3 kg/3 lb

1 onion, quartered

1 unwaxed lemon, quartered

15 g/½ oz fresh parsley stalks

1 tsp coriander seeds

1 cinnamon stick

pinch of sea salt

pinch of pepper

1. To make the stock, put the chicken, onion, lemon, parsley stalks, coriander seeds and cinnamon stick in a deep saucepan and pour in just enough water to cover. Bring to the boil, then reduce the heat to medium–low, cover and simmer for 1 hour, or until the chicken is almost falling off the bone. To check it is cooked, pierce the thickest part of the thigh with a skewer. Any juices should be piping hot and clear with no traces of red or pink.

2. Transfer the chicken to a large plate and leave to cool slightly. Meanwhile, simmer the broth until it has reduced to about 1.2 litres/2 pints. Season with the salt and pepper, then sieve into a jug. Remove the skin from the chicken and tear the flesh into strips.

3. Heat the oil in a heavy-based saucepan over a medium heat. Add the onions and chilli and fry for 2–3 minutes, stirring often. Stir in the cumin, paprika, sugar, mint and tomato purée, then pour in the broth. Bring to the boil, then gradually stir in the couscous. Reduce the heat to medium–low and simmer for 15 minutes. Stir in the cooked chicken strips and simmer for 5 minutes.

4. Serve the soup in shallow bowls, garnished with the coriander, with lemon wedges for squeezing over.

SPICY LENTIL &
CARROT SOUP

SERVES: 4	PREP TIME: 15 mins	COOK TIME: 45–50 mins

RED LENTILS ARE A GOOD SOURCE OF PROTEIN AND THE PERFECT VESSEL FOR ABSORBING STRONG, SPICY FLAVOURS.

INGREDIENTS

125 g/4½ oz split red lentils

1.2 litres/2 pints vegetable stock

350 g/12 oz carrots, sliced

2 onions, chopped

225 g/8 oz canned
chopped tomatoes

2 garlic cloves, chopped

2 tbsp oil

1 tsp ground cumin

1 tsp ground coriander

1 fresh green chilli, deseeded
and chopped

½ tsp ground turmeric

1 tbsp lemon juice

300 ml/10 fl oz milk

2 tbsp chopped fresh coriander

salt and pepper (optional)

TO SERVE

4 tsp natural yogurt

naan bread

spicy poppadums

1. Place the lentils in a large saucepan, together with 900 ml/1½ pints of the stock, the carrots, onions, tomatoes and garlic. Bring the mixture to the boil, then reduce the heat, cover and simmer for 30 minutes, or until the vegetables and lentils are tender.

2. Meanwhile, heat the oil in a separate saucepan. Add the cumin, ground coriander, chilli and turmeric and fry over a low heat for 1 minute. Remove from the heat and stir in the lemon juice. Season to taste with salt, if using.

3. Remove the soup from the heat and leave to cool slightly. Transfer to a food processor or blender, in batches if necessary, and process until smooth. Return the soup to the rinsed-out pan, add the spice mixture and the remaining stock and simmer over a low heat for 10 minutes.

4. Add the milk, taste and adjust the seasoning, adding salt and pepper if using. Stir in the chopped coriander and reheat gently; do not boil. Ladle into warmed bowls and serve immediately with yogurt, naan bread and spicy poppadums.

SPICY CHICKPEA
RED PEPPER SOUP

SERVES: 4	PREP TIME: 15 mins	COOK TIME: 25 mins

CHICKPEAS HAVE BEEN SHOWN TO HELP REGULATE BLOOD SUGAR AND IMPROVE
SATIETY AFTER A MEAL, MAKING THEM A USEFUL INGREDIENT IN THIS TASTY SOUP.

INGREDIENTS

2½ tbsp olive oil

6 spring onions, chopped

1 large fresh red jalapeño chilli,
deseeded and finely sliced

4 garlic cloves, finely chopped

2 tsp ground cumin

1 tsp chilli powder

3 fresh ripe tomatoes, peeled
and roughly chopped

400 g/14 oz ready-roasted
red peppers in water, drained
and thinly sliced

1 tbsp red pepper pesto

1 litre/1¾ pints reduced-salt
vegetable stock

400 g/14 oz canned chickpeas,
drained and rinsed

1 tsp stevia granules

2 tsp red wine vinegar

100 g/3½ oz baby spinach leaves

pepper (optional)

4 slices oat bread, about
40 g/1½ oz each, to serve

1. Heat the oil in a large saucepan over a medium heat. Add the spring onions and cook for 2–3 minutes, stirring occasionally, until soft.

2. Add the chilli, garlic, cumin and chilli powder and cook for 1 minute, stirring.

3. Stir in the tomatoes, red peppers, pesto and stock and bring to a simmer. Cook for 10 minutes, then add the chickpeas, stevia granules, vinegar and pepper, if using, and cook for a further 5 minutes.

4. Stir in the spinach and cook for 1 minute, until the spinach wilts. Serve with the oat bread.

VEGETABLE NOODLE BROTH

| SERVES: 4 | PREP TIME: 25–30 mins | COOK TIME: 25–30 minutes |

THIS HEARTY VEGETARIAN VERSION OF A POPULAR NOODLE-BASED BROTH IS A GOOD EXAMPLE OF THE INFLUENCE OF TIBETAN CUISINE IN THE BENGAL REGION. THE BROTH IS A GREAT FAVOURITE WITH STUDENTS.

INGREDIENTS

400 g/14 oz dried thick egg noodles
2 tbsp vegetable or groundnut oil
1 onion, finely chopped
1 tsp ground cumin
½ tsp ground turmeric
2 garlic cloves, crushed
2 tsp grated fresh ginger
1 tsp salt
2 fresh green chillies, finely chopped
100 g/3½ oz mangetout, thinly sliced lengthways
2 large carrots, cut into matchsticks
1 red pepper, deseeded and thinly sliced
2 tomatoes, finely chopped
2 tbsp dark soy sauce
1 litre/1¾ pints vegetable stock
1 tsp pepper
200 g/7 oz baby spinach leaves
6 tbsp finely chopped fresh coriander
1 tsp toasted sesame oil

1. Cook the noodles according to the packet instructions. Drain, rinse with cold water and set aside.

2. Meanwhile, heat the vegetable oil in a large saucepan over a medium heat. Add the onion and stir-fry for 8–10 minutes, or until lightly browned.

3. Add the cumin, turmeric, garlic, ginger, salt and chillies to the pan and stir-fry for 1–2 minutes. Add the mangetout, carrots and red pepper and stir-fry for a further 1–2 minutes.

4. Add the tomatoes, soy sauce, stock and pepper. Bring to the boil, then reduce the heat and simmer for 10–12 minutes, until the vegetables are tender.

5. Add the reserved noodles and the spinach and bring back to the boil. Stir until the spinach wilts, then remove from the heat and stir in the chopped coriander and sesame oil. Ladle into bowls and serve immediately.

HOT & SOUR
COURGETTES

SERVES: 4	PREP TIME: 15 mins, plus draining	COOK TIME: 5 mins

THIS SIMPLE DISH HAS A MEDIUM HOT PUNCH OF TASTY APACHE CHILLI. THE COURGETTES CAN BE PREPARED AS A VEGETABLE SIDE SERVING OR AS A DELICIOUS LIGHT SNACK WITH CRUSTY BREAD OR SESAME NOODLES.

INGREDIENTS

2 large courgettes, thinly sliced

1 tsp salt

2 tbsp groundnut oil

1 tsp Szechuan peppercorns, crushed

1 red Apache chilli, deseeded and sliced into thin strips

1 large garlic clove, thinly sliced

½ tsp finely chopped fresh ginger

1 tbsp rice vinegar

1 tbsp light soy sauce

2 tsp sugar

1 spring onion, green part included, thinly sliced

a few drops of sesame oil, to garnish

1 tsp sesame seeds, to garnish

1. Put the courgette slices in a large colander and toss with the salt. Cover with a plate and put a weight on top. Leave to drain for 20 minutes. Rinse off the salt and spread out the slices on kitchen paper to dry.

2. Preheat a wok over a high heat and add the groundnut oil. Add the peppercorns, chilli, garlic and ginger. Fry for about 20 seconds until the garlic is just beginning to colour.

3. Add the courgette slices and toss in the oil. Add the rice vinegar, soy sauce and sugar and stir-fry for 2 minutes. Add the spring onion and fry for 30 seconds. Garnish with the sesame oil and sesame seeds and serve immediately.

PREPARING CHILLIES

Chillies, especially the hotter ones, need to be handled with care as the capsaicin, which creates the heat, can be an irritant. They can also be soaked or toasted to enhance the flavour and make them easier to use.

Managing chilli heat

It is the capsaicin in a chilli that provides the heat and, as a rule, the smaller and thinner a chilli is, the hotter it will taste. A chilli's capsaicin is produced in a gland running down the middle of the fruit and this is the hottest part, although the seeds themselves are not that hot. If you deseed the chilli and remove the membrane you can reduce the heat.

Capsaicin is an oil and will stick to your skin, so be careful when chopping chillies, especially if you are removing the gland or the seeds. If your skin is sensitive, wear plastic gloves and never touch your eyes or mouth after handling chillies without thoroughly washing your hands first with soap and water. You can also protect your hands by rubbing them first with vegetable oil, which acts as an effective barrier.

Pan-frying chillies can also release a potent vapour that may irritate your eyes, so set the extractor to high before starting, or open a window.

If the heat of a chilli is too much in your mouth, don't drink a glass of water, which spreads the heat around. Reach instead for milk or yogurt as dairy ingredients help to dilute the heat more effectively.

Toasting chillies

Toasting both fresh and dried chillies endows them with a depth of flavour that will create a much richer final dish. To toast chillies, fry them in a dry frying pan over a medium heat until you can smell their aroma. Press large chillies, such as guajillos and pasillas, with a metal spatula against the hot surface until they puff up and soften. Smaller chillies, such as pequin, should be stirred constantly so they don't burn. You want blackened and blistered skins, but don't over-toast them or they will taste bitter. Immediately remove them from the pan and set aside.

Another technique is to put the chillies on a baking tray in an oven, preheated to 220°C/425°F/ Gas Mark 7, for 5 minutes, or until the chillies slightly puff up and soften.

Soaking chillies

Many recipes specify soaking chillies so they are soft enough to blend. This can soften fresh chillies or rehydrate dried ones. Do this by putting the chillies in a heatproof bowl and pouring over enough boiling water to cover. Leave to stand for 5 minutes, until the chillies are softened and flexible. Smaller chillies, such as bird's eye and chipotle, need to be weighted down with a small saucepan lid or heatproof plate to keep them submerged. Strain the chillies well, then pat dry and remove the stalks. If you want to reduce the heat of the chillies, deseed and devein them before soaking.

Never throw away the liquid you soak your chillies in. It is full of flavour and is great for giving a kick to soups, stews and gravies. Leave it to cool, then transfer to an airtight container and store in the fridge. Or for the really organised, freeze in an ice-cube tray, then transfer the individual cubes to a freezer-proof bag.

CHILLI SQUID
WITH WATERCRESS

| **SERVES:** 4 | **PREP TIME:** 4 mins, plus chilling | **COOK TIME:** 4 minutes |

HERE IS A SALAD THAT IS BOTH COOL AND HOT, CONSISTING OF FRESH SALAD LEAVES, STIR-FRIED SQUID AND FIERY BIRD'S EYE CHILLIES.

INGREDIENTS

12 squid tubes and tentacles, about 700 g/1 lb 9 oz total weight, cleaned and prepared

2–3 tbsp olive oil

2 bird's eye red chillies, deseeded and thinly sliced

2 spring onions, finely chopped

lemon wedges, for squeezing, plus extra to serve

3 handfuls of watercress

2 handfuls of baby spinach or rocket

freshly ground black pepper (optional)

DRESSING

100 ml/3½ fl oz olive oil

juice of a lime

2 shallots, thinly sliced

1 medium tomato, peeled, deseeded and finely chopped

1 garlic clove, crushed

freshly ground black pepper

1. To make the dressing, mix the oil, lime juice, shallots, tomato and garlic together in a bowl, season to taste with pepper, then cover and refrigerate until required.

2. Cut the squid tubes into 5-cm/2-inch pieces, then lightly score diamond patterns across the flesh with the tip of a sharp knife. Heat the oil in a wok or large frying pan over a high heat, add the squid pieces and tentacles and stir-fry for 1 minute. Add the chillies and spring onions and stir-fry for a further minute. Season to taste with pepper, if using, and add a good squeeze of lemon juice.

3. Mix the watercress and spinach together, then toss with enough of the dressing to coat lightly. Serve immediately with the squid, together with lemon wedges to squeeze over the dish.

TIP
CHOOSE FRESH, OPEN BUNCHES OF WATERCRESS RATHER THAN THOSE THAT ARE PACKAGED IN SEALED BAGS.

AUBERGINE PAPRIKA SALAD

SERVES: 4	PREP TIME: 15 mins	COOK TIME: 20 mins

THIS WARM SALAD IS A SATISFYING WAY TO EAT AUBERGINES, BRINGING YOU SMOKY FLAVOURS, A VARIETY OF TEXTURES AND WARMING SPICES ALL TOGETHER ON THE SAME PLATE.

INGREDIENTS

2 aubergines

2 tbsp olive oil

2 red peppers, deseeded and cut into 6 pieces each

400 g/14 oz canned chickpeas, drained and rinsed

1 red onion, finely chopped

4 wholemeal pittas, to serve

DRESSING

3 tbsp olive oil

juice of ½ lemon

1 tsp ground coriander

1 tsp ground cumin

2 tsp smoked paprika

1 tsp sugar

small bunch of fresh coriander, leaves removed and reserved and stalks chopped

salt and pepper (optional)

1. Preheat the grill to high. Cut the aubergines lengthways into 1-cm/½-inch thick slices, brush with oil on both sides and arrange on a grill rack. Add the red pepper pieces. Cook under the preheated grill until the aubergines are charred in patches on the top side; turn over and cook until the aubergines are soft and the red pepper pieces are lightly cooked and slightly brown in places. Remove from the heat but do not switch off the grill. Cut the aubergine slices into large bite-sized pieces and put into a shallow serving dish with the red pepper pieces, chickpeas and red onion.

2. To make the dressing, combine the oil, lemon juice, ground coriander, cumin, paprika and sugar with salt and pepper, if using, in a small bowl. Add the coriander stalks to the dressing and stir to combine. Spoon the dressing evenly over the salad and stir – it's best to do this while the vegetables are still warm.

3. Meanwhile, lightly toast the pittas under the grill.

4. Scatter the salad with the reserved coriander leaves and serve with the pittas.

SHAKSHUKA EGGS
WITH SPICY TOMATO SAUCE

SERVES: 4	PREP TIME: 10 mins	COOK TIME: 35 mins

ORIGINATING IN NORTH AFRICA, SHAKSHUKA IS A WARMING AND TASTY BREAKFAST DISH. IT IS DELICIOUS SERVED WITH A HUNK OF CRUSTY BREAD TO MOP UP THE JUICES.

INGREDIENTS

1 tsp cumin seeds
1 tsp coriander seeds
2 tsp olive oil
1 onion, finely chopped
600 g/1 lb 5 oz canned plum tomatoes
40 g/1½ oz chilli pesto
pinch of saffron
¼ tsp cayenne pepper
½ tsp salt
1 tsp pepper
3 tbsp chopped fresh coriander
4 large eggs

1. Crush the cumin seeds and coriander seeds. Place a non-stick frying pan over a medium heat and add the seeds to the pan. Stir for 1 minute, or until their aromas are released.

2. Reduce the heat to medium-low, add the oil and heat. Add the onion and cook, stirring occasionally, for 5 minutes, or until the onion is soft and just turning slightly golden.

3. Add the tomatoes, breaking up any large ones, pesto, saffron, cayenne pepper, and salt and pepper. Stir well, bring to a simmer and cook for 15 minutes, adding a little hot water towards the end if the pan looks too dry (but you don't want the sauce to be too runny). Stir in half of the fresh coriander.

4. Make four wells in the sauce and break an egg into each one. Cover the pan and cook over a low heat for 10 minutes, or until the egg whites are set but the yolk is still runny. Sprinkle the remaining fresh coriander over the top and serve immediately.

AVOCADO, BACON &
CHILLI FRITTATA

| SERVES: 4 | PREP TIME: 15 mins | COOK TIME: 14 mins |

INSPIRED BY THE MEXICAN FLAVOURS OF CHILLIES AND AVOCADO, THIS PROTEIN-PACKED FRITTATA IS LOVELY LINGERED OVER ON A LAZY MORNING. YOU CAN MAKE IT AHEAD AND STORE IT IN THE REFRIGERATOR FOR TWO DAYS.

INGREDIENTS

1 tbsp vegetable oil

8 streaky bacon rashers, roughly chopped

6 eggs, beaten

3 tbsp double cream

2 large avocados, peeled, stoned and sliced

1 fresh red Mexican poblano chilli (or, for a hotter option, 1 serrano), deseeded and thinly sliced

½ lime

sea salt and pepper (optional)

1. Preheat the grill to medium. Heat the oil in a 20-cm/8-inch ovenproof frying pan over a medium heat. Add the bacon and fry, stirring, for 4–5 minutes, or until crisp and golden. Using a slotted spoon, transfer to a plate lined with kitchen paper. Remove the pan from the heat.

2. Pour the eggs into a bowl, add the cream and season with salt and pepper, if using, then beat. Return the pan to the heat. When it is hot, pour in the egg mixture and cook for 1–2 minutes, without stirring. Sprinkle the bacon and avocado on top and cook for a further 2–3 minutes, or until the frittata is almost set and the underside is golden brown.

3. Place the frittata under the grill and cook for 3–4 minutes, or until the top is golden brown and the egg is set. Scatter with the chilli and squeeze the juice of the lime half over the top. Cut into wedges and serve.

TIP
THE SOFT TEXTURE OF THE FRITTATA WORKS BEST WITH REALLY CRISPY BACON, SO COOK THE BACON OVER A MEDIUM HEAT UNTIL IT HAS A DARK GOLDEN COLOUR.

EGG WHITE OMELETTE
WITH SPICY FILLING

SERVES: 1	PREP TIME: 10 mins	COOK TIME: 10 mins

RICH IN PROTEIN AND FIBRE, AN EGG WHITE OMELETTE IS AN EASY AND SATISFYING LUNCH, ESPECIALLY WHEN STUFFED WITH A TASTY, SPICY FILLING.

INGREDIENTS

4 egg whites

¼ tsp salt

1 tbsp water

2 tsp oil from a jar of semi-dried tomatoes

2 spring onions, finely chopped

85 g/3 oz canned mixed beans, rinsed

40 g/1½ oz frozen sweetcorn, thawed

50 ml/1¾ fl oz hot tomato salsa

3 sunblush tomatoes in oil, drained and chopped

½ tsp smoked paprika

½ tsp pepper

2 tbsp chopped fresh coriander

5 sprays cooking oil spray

1. Put the egg whites into a bowl with the salt and water and beat together.

2. Place the oil in a small frying pan over a medium heat. Add the spring onion and fry for 1 minute, until soft.

3. Add the beans and sweetcorn to the pan with the tomato salsa, tomatoes, paprika and pepper. Cook for a few minutes, then stir in half of the coriander. Set the mixture aside and keep warm.

4. Spray a separate small frying pan with the cooking oil spray and heat over a high heat until very hot. Pour in the egg white mixture and cook, making sure that the egg cooks evenly. When the underside is golden and the top is cooked but still moist, spoon the bean filling over the top then sprinkle over the remaining chopped coriander.

5. Tip the pan gently to one side, fold the omelette in half and slide out onto a warmed serving plate. Serve immediately.

STUFFED CHILLI BHAJIS

MAKES: 8	PREP TIME: 20 mins, plus soaking	COOK TIME: 10 mins

THIS SNACK OF CHILLIES STUFFED WITH A SPICED POTATO MIXTURE IS A CENTRAL INDIAN SPECIALITY, AND IS CLASSIC STREET FOOD. SERVE IT WITH YOUR FAVOURITE CHUTNEY OR NATURAL YOGURT.

INGREDIENTS

8 large, mild fresh green chillies

vegetable or groundnut oil, for deep-frying batter

250 g/9 oz gram flour

125 g/4½ oz rice flour

½ tsp baking powder

1 tsp ground cumin

2 tsp salt

1 tsp chilli powder

about 750 ml/1¼ pints cold water

STUFFING

2 tbsp vegetable or groundnut oil

1 tsp fennel seeds

2 tsp black mustard seeds

1 tsp cumin seeds

1 potato, peeled, boiled and mashed

3 tbsp finely chopped fresh coriander

1 tsp salt

½ tsp tamarind paste

1 tbsp roasted peanuts, roughly chopped

1. Slit the chillies lengthways and remove all the seeds using a small teaspoon. Soak the chillies in boiling water for 5 minutes. Drain on kitchen paper and set aside.

2. Mix together the batter ingredients with enough of the water to make a thin batter with the consistency of double cream. Set aside.

3. To make the stuffing, heat the oil in a pan. Add the fennel seeds, mustard seeds and cumin seeds. When the seeds start to pop, add the potato, coriander and salt and mix well. Add the tamarind paste and sprinkle over the roasted peanuts. Remove from the heat and mash until evenly combined.

4. Using your fingers, stuff the green chillies with the potato mixture.

5. Heat enough oil for deep-frying in a large saucepan or deep-fryer to 180–190°C/350–375°F, or until a cube of bread browns in 30 seconds. Working in batches, dip the stuffed green chillies in the batter and deep-fry, for 2–3 minutes, or until crisp and golden. Remove with a slotted spoon and drain on kitchen paper. Serve warm.

FIERY FISH FINGER
SANDWICH

SERVES: 2	PREP TIME: 10 mins	COOK TIME: 10 mins

FOR AN INSTANT FIERY SNACK, PREPARE SOME STANDARD FISH FINGERS, INFUSE THEM WITH RUSSIAN DRESSING THAT HAS CREAMED HORSERADISH, SRIRACHA HOT CHILLI SAUCE, WORCESTERSHIRE SAUCE AND PAPRIKA AS KEY INGREDIENTS.

INGREDIENTS

oil for deep-frying
20 fish fingers
4 large slices white bread
100 g/3½ oz rocket

RUSSIAN DRESSING

2 tbsp mayonnaise
1 tbsp creamed horseradish
1 tbsp tomato ketchup
1 tbsp soured cream
1 tbsp sriracha hot chilli sauce
1 tsp Worcestershire sauce
½ tsp smoked paprika

1. Heat enough oil for deep-frying in a large pan or deep-fryer to 180–190°C/350–375°F, or until a cube of bread browns in 30 seconds.

2. Meanwhile, mix together all of the Russian dressing ingredients in a small bowl and set aside.

3. Deep-fry the fish fingers in batches of 10 for 5 minutes or until golden, then remove with a slotted spoon, drain on kitchen paper and leave in a warm place while you cook the remaining fish fingers.

4. Spread some of the dressing on 2 of the bread slices. Divide the fish fingers between two slices of bread and drizzle over the rest of the dressing. Top with the rocket and the remaining bread slices and serve immediately.

TURKEY
PAPRIKA TACOS

| SERVES: 4 | PREP TIME: 15 mins, plus marinating | COOK TIME: 8 mins |

TURKEY MAKES A REFRESHING CHANGE FROM CHICKEN IN ALMOST ANY DISH AND ITS SOMEWHAT RICHER FLAVOUR LENDS ITSELF WELL TO MEXICAN-STYLE MEALS SUCH AS THIS ONE.

INGREDIENTS

300 g/10½ oz skinless, boneless turkey breasts, cut into strips

2 garlic cloves, crushed

2 tsp smoked paprika

juice of ½ lime

1 red onion, chopped

1 tomato, chopped

100 g/3½ oz cooked black beans

100 g/3½ oz crisp lettuce, shredded

4 wholemeal tortillas

40 g/1½ oz reduced-fat Cheddar cheese, grated

2 tsp hot pepper sauce

100 g/3½ oz reduced-fat soured cream

1. Put the turkey strips in a shallow non-metallic bowl. Stir in the garlic with the paprika and lime juice. Cover and leave to marinate for 30 minutes.

2. Meanwhile, combine the onion, tomato, beans and lettuce in a bowl.

3. Preheat the grill to medium-hot. Line a baking tray with foil. Put the turkey strips on the prepared tray and cook under the preheated grill for about 6 minutes, turning once, until golden and cooked through. Set aside.

4. Heat the tortillas under the grill until slightly golden and crisp. Divide the turkey and the bean mixture evenly between the tortillas, arranging them on one half of the tortilla only. Scatter over the cheese and drizzle with the hot pepper sauce and soured cream. Fold the tacos to serve.

HOT SAUCES & RUBS

———————————

Add a fiery intensity to any dish with this diverse choice
of flaming sauces and rubs. The international range of
sauces, from Mexican salsa to Caribbean jerk sauce,
can be used as marinades or dips or can be served
alongside seafood and meat dishes. From Hot-as-Hell
Horseradish to Sweltering Satay and Ketchup with a
Kick, there's sure to be a sauce to set you on fire.

SPICY SALSA

MAKES: about 450 ml/15 fl oz	**PREP TIME:** 10 mins	**COOK TIME:** 20 mins

THIS SALSA PROVIDES A SPICY ACCOMPANIMENT TO ANY MEXICAN MEAL AND IS ESPECIALLY GOOD ON BURRITOS. THE FRESH TASTE OF THE CORIANDER, LIME JUICE AND ONION SUCCESSFULLY OFFSET THE HEAT OF THE JALAPEÑOS.

INGREDIENTS

vegetable oil spray
8 plum tomatoes, halved
2–4 jalapeños, to taste, halved, cored and deseeded
4 garlic cloves
1 large onion, cut into wedges
25 g/1 oz fresh coriander
4 tbsp lime juice
1 tsp salt

1. Preheat the oven to 230°C/450°F/Gas Mark 8 and spray a baking sheet with oil.

2. Place the tomatoes, jalapeños, garlic and onion on the prepared baking sheet and lightly spray with oil. Sprinkle with a little salt and roast in the preheated oven for about 15–20 minutes, until the vegetables soften and begin to brown.

3. Place the vegetables in a food processor and pulse to a chunky purée. Add the coriander, lime juice and 1 teaspoon of salt and pulse until the coriander is chopped and all of the ingredients are well combined.

4. To store, cover and refrigerate for up to 1 week.

RED-HOT
GARLIC & CHILLI OIL

MAKES: about 225 ml/8 fl oz	**PREP TIME:** 5 mins	**COOK TIME:** 2 hrs

CHILLI OIL CAN BE USED TO SPICE UP DISHES, WHETHER DRIZZLING OVER PIZZAS OR PASTA OR ADDING A SPLASH TO MEXICAN-STYLE BEEF CHILLIES. THE LONGER YOU LEAVE THE OIL TO SETTLE, THE HOTTER IT GETS!

INGREDIENTS

5 garlic cloves, halved lengthways

2 tbsp deseeded and chopped jalapeño chilli

1 tsp dried oregano

225 ml/8 fl oz rapeseed oil

1. Preheat the oven to 150°C/300°F/Gas Mark 2. Combine the garlic, chilli and oregano with the oil in an ovenproof glass measuring jug. Place on an ovenproof dish in the centre of the oven and heat for 1½–2 hours. The temperature of the oil should reach 120°C/250°F.

2. Remove from the oven, allow to cool, then strain through muslin into a clean jar. Store in an airtight container in the refrigerator for up to 1 month. You can also leave the garlic and chilli pieces in the oil and strain before using.

KETCHUP
WITH A KICK

MAKES: about 600 ml/1 pint	**PREP TIME**: 15 mins	**COOK TIME**: 2 hrs 15 mins

THIS IS A GREAT RECIPE FOR THE TIME WHEN TOMATOES ARE AT THEIR CHEAPEST AND MOST PLENTIFUL. MAKE UP LARGE BATCHES OF THIS KETCHUP AND ENJOY THE TASTE OF SUMMER ALL YEAR ROUND.

INGREDIENTS

2.25 kg/5 lb ripe, juicy tomatoes, roughly chopped

2 red jalapeño chillies, roughly chopped

1 sweet white onion, roughly chopped

1 tsp salt

1 tsp fennel seeds

1 tsp black mustard seeds

275 ml/9 fl oz cider vinegar or white wine vinegar

100 g/3½ oz soft light brown sugar

1 cinnamon stick

½ tsp ground nutmeg

½ tsp sweet paprika

1–3 tsp cayenne pepper

1–2 tbsp tomato purée (optional)

pepper (optional)

1. Put the tomatoes, chillies, onion and salt into a large saucepan over a high heat. Stir until the tomatoes begin to break down, then reduce the heat to low, cover and simmer for 30 minutes, or until the tomatoes are pulpy.

2. Meanwhile, put the fennel seeds and mustard seeds on a square of muslin, bring the sides together and tie to make a bag, then set aside.

3. Pass the tomato mixture through a sieve into a large saucepan, rubbing backwards and forwards with a wooden spoon and scraping the base of the sieve to produce as much purée as possible.

4. Add the spice bag and the vinegar, sugar, cinnamon stick, nutmeg, paprika and cayenne pepper. Season with pepper, if using, then stir until the sugar dissolves. Bring to the boil, then reduce the heat and simmer, uncovered, for 1½ hours, skimming the surface as necessary, until the sauce is reduced and thickened. Transfer to a bowl and leave to cool.

5. Depending on how well-flavoured the tomatoes were you might want to add some tomato purée. Remove the spice bag and cinnamon stick.

6. Leave the ketchup to cool completely. It can be used immediately, or stored in an airtight container in the refrigerator for up to 1 month. It can also be frozen for up to 3 months.

FIERY & FIERCE
GOCHUJANG SAUCE

| **MAKES:** about 150 ml/5 fl oz | **PREP TIME:** 5 mins | **COOK TIME:** none |

KOREAN COOKS USED TO MAKE ENOUGH GOCHUJANG, A FERMENTED CHILLI AND SOYBEAN PASTE, IN THE SPRING TO LAST A FAMILY ALL YEAR. USE THIS SAUCE AS A MARINADE OR DIPPING SAUCE, OR FOR BASTING MEAT AND POULTRY.

INGREDIENTS

5 tbsp gochujang paste
2 tsp chilli paste
2 tbsp sugar
2 tbsp hot water
2 tsp light soy sauce
1 tsp rice vinegar
1 tsp toasted sesame oil

1. Combine the gochujang paste, chilli paste and sugar in a heatproof bowl, then add the water, stirring to blend and dissolve the sugar and paste.

2. Stir in the soy sauce, vinegar and sesame oil. Leave the sauce to cool completely.

3. The sauce can be used immediately, or stored in an airtight container in the refrigerator for up to 2 weeks.

TIP
THIS RECIPE COMBINES AUTHENTIC FLAVOUR WITH THE SPEED OF USING READY-MADE FERMENTED BEAN AND CHILLI PASTE.

INTENSE TEXAN
CHILLI SAUCE

| **MAKES:** about 750 ml/1¼ pints | **PREP TIME:** 10 mins | **COOK TIME:** 25 mins |

TEXAN CHILLI – OR "BIG RED" AS THE LOCALS KNOW IT – IS NOT MADE WITH BEANS, JUST MEAT, SO IT NEEDS A TASTY SAUCE LIKE THIS THAT HAS PLENTY OF HEAT AND FLAVOUR.

INGREDIENTS

2 tbsp sunflower oil or rapeseed oil

1 red onion, chopped

2 large garlic cloves, chopped

1 green serrano chilli, halved lengthways

1 tbsp soft dark brown sugar

2 tsp ground cumin

2 tsp dried Mexican oregano or dried thyme

2 dried morita chipotle chillies, toasted, soaked, deseeded and chopped

1 dried guajillo chilli, toasted, soaked, deseeded and chopped

1 dried New Mexico red chilli, toasted, soaked, deseeded and chopped

400 g/14 oz canned chopped tomatoes

125 ml/4 fl oz beef stock

125 ml/4 fl oz strong black coffee

salt and pepper (optional)

1. Heat the oil in a saucepan over a medium-high heat. Add the onion and fry for 3–5 minutes, or until soft. Add the garlic, serrano chilli, sugar, cumin and oregano and fry for a further minute.

2. Transfer the onion mixture to a food processor or blender. Add the chipotle chillies, guajillo chilli and New Mexico chilli, tomatoes, stock and coffee and season with salt and pepper, if using. Process until puréed, scraping down the side of the processor as necessary.

3. Transfer the purée to the pan and bring to the boil. Reduce the heat to low, cover and simmer for 15 minutes, stirring occasionally.

4. The sauce can be used immediately, or left to cool and stored in an airtight container in the refrigerator for up to 3 days. This sauce can be frozen for up to 3 months.

TEXAS-STYLE
CHILLI

SERVES: 4	PREP TIME: 10 mins	COOK TIME: 3 hrs

TEXANS DON'T TOLERATE BEANS OR ANY OTHER ADDITIONS IN THEIR BIG BOWLS OF CHILLI. WHAT YOU SEE IS WHAT YOU GET – JUST CHUNKS OF BEEF AND HOT CHILLI SAUCE. IT'S PLAIN AND SIMPLE, AND UTTERLY DELICIOUS.

INGREDIENTS

2 tbsp rendered bacon fat, sunflower oil or rapeseed oil, plus extra, if needed

750 g/1 lb 10 oz stewing steak, cut into 2.5-cm/1-inch cubes

1 large onion, finely chopped

1 large garlic clove, finely chopped

1 tbsp dried red chilli flakes

750 ml/1¼ pints Intense Texan Chilli Sauce (see previous page)

1 tbsp masa harina

1 tbsp red wine vinegar

salt and pepper (optional)

cooked rice and soured cream, to serve

1. Heat the fat in a large, heavy-based saucepan over a medium heat. Season the beef to taste with salt and pepper, if using. Working in batches, add the beef to the pan and fry, stirring occasionally, until brown on all sides, adding extra fat as needed. Set aside the beef and juices.

2. Pour off all but 1 tablespoon of the fat. Add the onion to the pan and fry for 3–5 minutes, or until soft. Add the garlic and chilli flakes and fry for a further minute. Return the beef and all the juices to the pan and stir in the Texan Sauce. Cover and bring to the boil, then reduce the heat to low and simmer for 2¼–2½ hours, until the beef is tender.

3. Put the harina into a small bowl and stir in the vinegar. Stir the mixture into the chilli and simmer for 10 minutes, or until the chilli thickens. Season to taste. Serve in bowls over rice, with soured cream.

CHIMICHURRI
SWELTERING SAUCE

| **MAKES:** about 175 ml/6 fl oz | **PREP TIME:** 5 mins, plus marinating | **COOK TIME:** none |

NO LATIN AMERICAN BARBECUE IS COMPLETE WITHOUT A BOWL OF ZINGY, FRESH CHIMICHURRI, A BLEND OF HERBS AND CHILLIES. THIS HOT AND SPICY VERSION HAS A BIRD'S EYE CHILLI TO CRANK UP THE HEAT. SERVE WITH ALL GRILLED AND ROASTED MEATS OR A SELECTION OF CRUDITÉS.

INGREDIENTS

30 g/1 oz fresh coriander leaves
30 g/1 oz fresh flat-leaf parsley leaves
4 garlic cloves, roughly chopped
1–2 green bird's eye chillies, finely chopped
1 tsp dried chilli flakes
1 tsp dried Mexican oregano or 1 tsp dried thyme (optional)
125 ml/4 fl oz sunflower oil or rapeseed oil
4 tbsp red wine vinegar or white wine vinegar
salt and pepper

1. Put the coriander, parsley, garlic, chillies, chilli flakes, oregano, if using, and salt and pepper to taste into a food processor and finely chop, scraping down the sides, as necessary. Do not blend to a purée.

2. With the motor running, slowly drizzle in the oil. Add the vinegar and adjust the seasoning if necessary.

3. The sauce can be used immediately, but is best if stored in an airtight container in the refrigerator for at least 3 hours to allow the flavours to blend. The sauce will keep for up to 3 days in the refrigerator if covered with an extra layer of oil, although its bright-green colour will dull. Pour off the oil before serving.

TIP
IF YOU DON'T WANT TO USE A FOOD PROCESSOR, FINELY CHOP THE CORIANDER, PARSLEY AND GARLIC, THEN MIX TOGETHER IN A NON-METALLIC BOWL.

JAMAICAN JERK
SAUCE

MAKES: about 300 ml/10 fl oz	**PREP TIME:** 10 mins, plus marinating	**COOK TIME:** none

THIS HOT, HOT, HOT CARIBBEAN FAVOURITE CAN BE USED AS A MARINADE OR AS A BASTING SAUCE WHILE BARBECUING. CHICKEN IS ITS TRADITIONAL PARTNER, BUT IT ALSO ADDS A SUNNY CARIBBEAN TASTE TO MOST MEAT AND SEAFOOD DISHES.

INGREDIENTS

4 tbsp freshly squeezed lemon juice

4 tbsp dark soy sauce

4 tbsp sunflower oil

4 tbsp red wine vinegar or white wine vinegar

4 red Scotch bonnet chillies or habañero chillies, deseeded and very finely chopped

4 spring onions, very finely chopped

1 shallot, very finely chopped

2.5-cm/1-inch piece fresh ginger, grated

2 tbsp soft light brown sugar

2 tsp dried thyme

1 tsp ground allspice

½ tsp ground cinnamon

¼ tsp ground cloves

salt and pepper

1. Mix together the lemon juice, soy sauce, oil and vinegar in a large non-metallic bowl.

2. Stir in the remaining ingredients and season to taste with salt and pepper, stirring until the sugar dissolves. Set aside for at least 30 minutes for the flavours to blend.

3. The sauce can be used immediately, or stored in an airtight container in the refrigerator for up to 1 month.

JERK CHICKEN

| SERVES: 4 | PREP TIME: 10 mins, plus marinating | COOK TIME: 40 mins |

AUTHENTIC JAMAICAN JERK CHICKEN HAS A UNIQUE FLAVOUR FROM BEING SLOWLY COOKED OVER PIMENTO, OR ALLSPICE, WOOD. WHILE THE FLAVOUR HERE ISN'T EXACTLY THE SAME, IT DOES GIVES YOU THE JAMAICAN JERK HEAT.

INGREDIENTS

4 chicken legs

300 ml/10 fl oz Jamaican Jerk Sauce (see previous page)

sunflower oil, for brushing

coleslaw, pineapple and rice salad, to serve (optional)

1. Use a fork to pierce the chicken legs all over. Place the chicken in a bowl in a single layer. Pour over the Jamaican Jerk Sauce and rub into the chicken pieces. Cover the bowl with clingfilm and marinate in the refrigerator for at least 4 hours, or for up to 36 hours.

2. Remove the chicken from the refrigerator 30 minutes in advance of cooking. Light a barbecue and heat until the coals turn grey. Alternatively, preheat the grill to high and oil the grill rack.

3. Place the chicken pieces on the rack, fleshy-side down. Brush with some of the sauce remaining in the bowl and cook for 20 minutes.

4. Turn the chicken over and cook for a further 20 minutes, brushing with the remaining sauce, or until it is cooked all the way through and the juices run clear when the thickest part of the flesh is pierced with a sharp knife.

5. Transfer the chicken to a warmed plate and leave to rest for 5 minutes. Use a cleaver to cut each leg into 4 pieces, then serve with coleslaw, pineapple and rice salad, if using.

LOUISIANA
HOT PEPPER SAUCE

| **MAKES:** about 125 ml/4 fl oz | **PREP TIME:** 5 mins | **COOK TIME:** 15 mins |

THIS SAUCE IS TRADITIONALLY MADE WITH FRESH, SMALL TABASCO CHILLIES BUT THEY
CAN BE DIFFICULT TO SOURCE, SO DRIED CAYENNE OR BIRD'S EYE CHILLIES ARE USED
IN THIS RECIPE TO GIVE THE SAME TONGUE-TINGLING SENSATION.

INGREDIENTS

55 g/2 oz dried red cayenne peppers
or dried red bird's eye chillies,
stems removed, very roughly
chopped and soaked for
30 minutes
125 ml/4 fl oz white wine vinegar
½ tsp salt

1. Turn the extractor to high or open a window. Drain the soaked chillies. Put the chillies, vinegar and salt into a small saucepan. Cover the pan and bring to the boil, then reduce the heat to low and simmer for 10–12 minutes, or until very soft.

2. Tip the contents of the pan into a small food processor or blender and purée, scraping down the side of the processor as necessary. Strain the blended mixture to remove the seeds. Transfer the sauce to a non-metallic bowl and leave to cool completely.

3. Leave the sauce to mature for at least 2 weeks in an airtight container in the refrigerator before using. The sauce will then keep in the refrigerator for a further month.

PIQUANT PICO DE GALLO SAUCE

MAKES: about 175 ml/6 fl oz	**PREP TIME:** 10 mins, plus resting	**COOK TIME:** none

HOT AND FRESH FLAVOURS MINGLE IN THIS SIMPLE MEXICAN SALSA-LIKE SAUCE, WHICH ADDS A BURST OF CHILLI HEAT TO EVERYTHING FROM A BOWL OF TORTILLA CHIPS TO GRILLED MEAT AND TACOS.

INGREDIENTS

150 ml/5 fl oz passata

2 tbsp freshly squeezed lime juice or orange juice, or to taste

2 large pickled garlic cloves or fresh garlic cloves, very finely chopped

½ sweet white onion, finely chopped

2 tbsp pickled jalapeño chillies, drained and finely chopped

½ tsp ancho chilli powder

salt and pepper (optional)

small handful of coriander leaves, finely chopped, to garnish

1. Combine the passata and lime juice in a non-metallic bowl and season with salt and pepper, if using. Add all the remaining ingredients, except the coriander leaves.

2. The sauce can be served immediately, but will benefit from being left to stand at room temperature for 30 minutes for the flavours to blend. Stir well before serving and adjust the lime juice and salt and pepper, if using. Sprinkle with coriander just before serving.

3. If there is any sauce left over, pour a layer of olive oil over it, cover and store in the refrigerator for up to 3 days. Stir in the oil just before serving and garnish with chopped fresh coriander.

TIP

STILL NOT HOT ENOUGH? THEN USE RED OR GREEN THAI CHILLIES INSTEAD OF THE JALAPEÑOS.

INGREDIENTS
FOR HOT SAUCES

With a bit of judicious selection, common storecupboard ingredients can produce an astonishing variety of flavours in your sauces. Use the ingredients below and experiment to suit your taste.

Chillies are the essential ingredient in most hot sauce recipes, and they come in a wide range of varieties and heats.

Harissa paste is a strong and aromatic dark-red paste (see opposite, above left) made from chillies, spices and herbs, used for adding heat and flavour to North African food. The base ingredients are chillies, garlic, oil, ground cumin, coriander and caraway seeds.

Herbs and spices provide a depth of flavour, whether they are fresh or dried. Jamaican Jerk Sauce, for example, wouldn't taste authentic without dried allspice, and Chimichurri Sweltering Sauce relies on a medley of fresh herbs.

Horseradish is a thick, white root which, when freshly grated, has an intense, sharp, hot flavour. Mixing grated horseradish with lemon juice helps prolong the sharpness. If buying grated horseradish, avoid horseradish sauce, which is mixed with cream, or grated horseradish in vinegar.

Mustard is one of the most popular and widely used spices and condiments and will add a hot punch to a meal. The level of heat is defined by the seed type and preparation. Choose dried bright-yellow mustard powder for the hottest flavour.

Paprika is the finely ground powder of dried sweet red peppers – its heat ranges from mild and sweet to intensely hot. It needs to be fresh; otherwise the flavour is lost.

Oil is essential for frying chillies and other ingredients and for adding body to sauces. Keep a selection – such as sunflower, rapeseed, groundnut and olive – to ring the flavour changes.

Salt is used to bring out individual flavours.

Sambal oelek paste is a red sauce (see opposite, below right) from Indonesia – it is made with chillies, salt and citrus juice or vinegar and comes in varying degrees of hotness and is sold in supermarkets and specialist food shops.

Sugars, both white and brown, provide a counterpoint to hot spiciness and act as a preservative. Always dissolve sugar before bringing a sauce to the boil to prevent crystals forming.

Szechuan peppercorns have an unmistakeable flavour – the heat blends with a lingering tingling sensation on your tongue and cheeks (see opposite, bottom left).

Vinegar provides a sour background, as well as acting as a preservative. Caribbean and many traditional North American sauces contain distilled white vinegar, but cider or red and white wine vinegars are also good.

Wasabi, also known as Japanese horseradish (see opposite, above right), comes from a root and packs quite a punch. It is pungent and hot, and sold as a stem for grating, ready-made as a paste or in powder form.

PERI-PERI
AT YOUR PERIL SAUCE

| MAKES: about 75 ml/2½ fl oz | PREP TIME: 10 mins | COOK TIME: 10 mins |

THIS PERI-PERI SAUCE IS AS GOOD AS ANY YOU WOULD FIND AT WELL-KNOWN RESTAURANTS! YOU CAN PAIR IT WITH FRIED CHICKEN WINGS TO CREATE A HOT AND SPICY MEAL.

INGREDIENTS

4 tbsp sunflower oil

24 peri-peri chillies or red bird's eye chillies, chopped

½ onion, finely chopped

4 large garlic cloves, chopped

1 tsp sweet paprika

¼ tsp ground allspice

6 tbsp freshly squeezed lemon juice, or to taste

2 tbsp water

finely grated zest of 1 lemon

salt and pepper (optional)

1. Turn the extractor to high or open a window to allow air to circulate. Heat the oil in a saucepan over a medium heat. Add the chillies and onion and fry for 3 minutes. Add the garlic, paprika and allspice and stir for a further minute.

2. Add 4 tablespoons of the lemon juice and the water and season with salt and pepper, if using. Bring to the boil, stirring. Reduce the heat to very low, cover and simmer for 5 minutes, or until the chillies are very soft. Uncover and check once or twice to make sure the garlic doesn't burn.

3. If you would like a smooth, restaurant-style sauce, transfer the ingredients to a small food processor or blender and purée, or leave as a chunky sauce, if preferred. Stir in the remaining lemon juice. Adjust the seasoning and lemon juice, as desired. Stir in the lemon zest.

4. The sauce can be used immediately, or left to cool completely and stored in an airtight container in the refrigerator for up to 2 weeks.

FIERY ROASTED TOMATO SAUCE

MAKES: about 175 ml/6 fl oz	PREP TIME: 10 mins	COOK TIME: 45 mins

THIS SAUCE, WITH ITS PAPRIKA AND SHERRY INGREDIENTS, HAS A SPANISH FLAVOUR AND IS GREAT WHEN SERVED AS A DIP WITH TORTILLA CHIPS OR AS AN ACCOMPANIMENT TO SPANISH OMELETTE AND CHIPS.

INGREDIENTS

6 vine-ripened tomatoes

1 red pepper, cut into quarters and deseeded

1 garlic clove, unpeeled

1 red onion, cut into quarters

4 tbsp olive oil

1 small red jalapeño chilli, very finely chopped

1 tsp hot paprika

1 tbsp sherry

salt and pepper

1. Preheat the oven to 180°C/350°F/Gas Mark 4.

2. Lay out the vegetables on a large baking tray, brush with olive oil, then roast in the oven, turning once halfway through cooking, for about 45 minutes or until they are blistered and slightly charred.

3. Leave to cool. When cool enough to handle, peel the tomatoes and red pepper, and squeeze the garlic from its skin. Transfer the tomato, red pepper, garlic flesh and onion to a food processor and process to a fairly smooth consistency.

4. Spoon the mixture into a large serving bowl and stir in the chilli, paprika and sherry. Season to taste. The sauce can be used immediately or left to cool completely and stored in an airtight container in the refrigerator for up to 1 week.

TIP

THE TABLESPOON OF SHERRY IN THIS RECIPE CAN ALSO BE REPLACED BY MADEIRA, WHICH IS A FORTIFIED WINE FROM PORTUGAL.

HABAÑERO
CHILLI RUB

MAKES: about 10 tbsp	**PREP TIME**: 10 mins, plus chilling	**COOK TIME**: none

THE HABANERO CHILLI IS ONE OF THE HOTTEST CHILLIES IN THE WORLD, RATED 100,000–350,000 ON THE SCOVILLE SCALE. SO IF YOU'RE CHOOSING TO USE THIS RUB, BE PREPARED FOR YOUR TASTEBUDS TO TINGLE!

INGREDIENTS

2 tbsp paprika
1–2 tbsp dried crushed habañero chillies or chilli powder
1 tbsp garlic powder
1 tbsp onion powder
1 tbsp ground cumin
1 tbsp salt
2 tsp pepper
2 tsp soft light brown sugar
1 tsp cayenne pepper
½ tsp freshly grated nutmeg

1. Mix all the ingredients together in a small bowl until thoroughly combined.

2. Rub the mixture thoroughly into meat, poultry, fish or seafood 1–2 hours before cooking.

3. Put in a shallow dish, cover tightly and chill in the refrigerator until required.

HOT-AS-HELL
HORSERADISH SAUCE

| MAKES: about 150 ml/5 fl oz | PREP TIME: 10 mins | COOK TIME: none |

THIS EASY SAUCE GETS ITS PUNCHY HEAT FROM FRESHLY GRATED HORSERADISH. IT'S TRADITIONALLY ADDED TO SEAFOOD COCKTAILS BUT YOU CAN ADD A SPOONFUL OR TWO TO HOME-MADE TOMATO SOUP FOR AN EXTRA KICK.

INGREDIENTS

125 g/4½ oz tomato ketchup, plus extra, if needed

2.5-cm/1-inch piece horseradish, finely grated, or 1 tbsp grated horseradish

1 tbsp freshly squeezed lemon juice, or to taste, plus extra if needed

pepper (optional)

1. Put the ketchup and horseradish into a bowl and stir to combine.

2. Add the lemon juice and pepper, if using. Stir to combine, then add extra lemon juice to taste.

3. The sauce can be served immediately, or stored in an airtight container in the refrigerator for up to 3 weeks. After 1–2 days the sauce will thicken, so you will need to beat in extra ketchup or lemon juice with a fork when ready to serve.

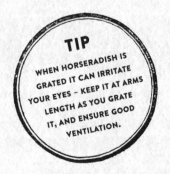

TIP

WHEN HORSERADISH IS GRATED IT CAN IRRITATE YOUR EYES – KEEP IT AT ARMS LENGTH AS YOU GRATE IT, AND ENSURE GOOD VENTILATION.

RAS EL HANOUT
CARIBBEAN RUB

| **MAKES**: about 7 tbsp | **PREP TIME**: 10 mins, plus chilling | **COOK TIME**: none |

COMBINED WITH OIL, THIS CARIBBEAN FAVOURITE CAN BE USED AS A MARINADE OR AS A BASTING SAUCE WHILE BARBECUING. CHICKEN IS ITS TRADITIONAL PARTNER, BUT IT ADDS A CARIBBEAN TASTE TO MEAT AND SEAFOOD DISHES.

INGREDIENTS

2 tsp ground cumin
2 tsp ground ginger
2 tsp ground turmeric
2 tsp ground cinnamon
2 tsp ground cardamom seeds
2 tsp ground coriander seeds
2 tsp ground ginger
2 tsp ground allspice
2 tsp saffron threads
1 tsp freshly grated nutmeg
1 tsp salt
1 tsp pepper
½ tsp ground cloves

1. Mix all the ingredients together in a small bowl until they are thoroughly combined.

2. Rub the mixture thoroughly into meat, poultry, fish or seafood just before cooking.

3. Put in a shallow dish, cover tightly and chill in the refrigerator until required.

RAS EL HANOUT
GARLIC & THYME
ROAST LEG OF LAMB

SERVES: 6–8	PREP TIME: 15 mins	COOK TIME: 3hrs 30 mins, plus resting

SLOW-ROASTING THIS SPICED LEG OF LAMB WILL GIVE YOU MELTINGLY TENDER MEAT, AND WILL FILL YOUR KITCHEN WITH WONDERFUL AROMAS.

INGREDIENTS

20 fresh lemon thyme sprigs

8 garlic cloves, peeled

4 tsp sea salt flakes

4 tbsp ras el hanout
(see previous page)

4 tbsp olive oil

1 leg of lamb, weighing 2–2.5 kg/4 lb
8 oz–5 lb 8 oz

2 heads of garlic, halved horizontally

2 onions, cut into quarters

300 ml/10 fl oz water

salt and pepper, to serve

1 tbsp Greek-style natural yogurt,
to serve

1. Preheat the oven to 150°C/300°F/Gas Mark 2. Strip the leaves from half the lemon thyme and put them in a pestle and mortar. Add the garlic cloves and 3 teaspoons of the salt and crush. Add the ras el hanout and oil, and mix to form a rough paste.

2. Put the lamb in a roasting tin. Using a sharp knife, make several small slits in the skin. Rub in the spice paste, working it into the slits well. Sprinkle over the remaining salt, put the halved heads of garlic and quartered onions alongside it, sprinkle over the remaining lemon thyme, then pour the water around it.

3. Roast for 30 minutes, uncovered. Baste the lamb with the cooking liquid and cover the tray with foil. Roast for a further 3 hours, basting every half an hour.

4. Transfer the lamb to a serving platter, add the onions and garlic and leave to rest, covered in foil, for 30 minutes.

5. For the gravy, skim the excess oil off the liquid and season with a pinch of salt and pepper. Stir the yogurt into the gravy and serve alongside the roast lamb and onions.

RED-HOT
GREEN SAUCE

MAKES: about 400 ml/14 fl oz	**PREP TIME**: 10 mins	**COOK TIME**: none

THIS COMBINATION OF PICKLED JALAPEÑOS AND SMOKED HOT PAPRIKA IS PACKED FULL OF PUNCH, MAKING READY-MADE SALSA SEEM MILD AND UNEXCEPTIONAL! THE SAUCE IS ZESTY AND HOT AND THE FRESH GREEN COLOUR LOOKS APPETIZING IN A CONTRASTING BOWL.

INGREDIENTS

450 g/1 lb canned tomatillos, drained, stem ends removed and roughly chopped

4 spring onions, chopped

2 large garlic cloves, roughly chopped

2 tbsp drained pickled jalapeño chillies, chopped

handful of coriander leaves

freshly squeezed lime juice (optional)

1 tsp clear honey, to taste

½ tsp hot smoked paprika

salt and pepper (optional)

1 tbsp finely chopped fresh coriander, to garnish

1. Put the tomatillos, spring onions, garlic, chillies and coriander leaves into a food processor and process in short blasts to finely chop, but not purée.

2. Transfer the mixture to a bowl. Season with salt and pepper, if using, then add the lime juice, if using, and the honey to taste. Stir in the paprika.

3. The sauce can be used immediately, or stored in an airtight container in the refrigerator for up to 4 days, although the colour will start to dull after 3 days. Sprinkle with the chopped coriander just before serving.

SWELTERING
SATAY SAUCE

SERVES: about 175 ml/6 fl oz	PREP TIME: 10 mins	COOK TIME: 5 mins

THE TRADITIONALLY MILD PEANUT SAUCE IS HEATED UP IN THIS VERSION WITH THE ADDITION OF AN INDONESIAN CHILLI PASTE CALLED SAMBAL OELEK. THIS IS SOLD IN MOST ASIAN FOOD SHOPS BUT THE INTENSITY OF THE HEAT VARIES WITH THE BRAND.

INGREDIENTS

2 tbsp sunflower oil

2 shallots, finely chopped

1 large garlic clove, finely chopped

2.5-cm/1-inch piece fresh ginger, finely chopped

1–3 tsp Indonesian chilli paste (sambal oelek)

100 g/3½ oz creamed coconut, dissolved in 250 ml/9 fl oz boiling water

5 tbsp crunchy peanut butter

1 tsp tamarind paste or freshly squeezed lime juice, or to taste

1 tsp dark soy sauce, or to taste

4 tbsp water, if needed

4 red jalapeño chillies, deseeded and thinly sliced

salt and pepper (optional)

1. Heat the oil in a wok over a high heat until very hot. Add the shallots, garlic and ginger and stir-fry for 1–2 minutes, or until the shallots are soft and just beginning to colour. Stir in the chilli paste and continue frying for a further 30 seconds.

2. Add the creamed coconut and peanut butter, stirring until blended. Stir in the tamarind paste and soy sauce, season to taste with pepper, if using, and continue stirring over a medium heat for 2–3 minutes. If the mixture looks separated, stir in the water and beat well. Stir in the chillies. Adjust the seasoning, if necessary, and add extra chilli paste, tamarind paste and soy sauce, to taste.

3. The sauce can be served hot or at room temperature, or left to cool completely and stored in an airtight container in the refrigerator for up to 1 week.

NACHO SAUCE

MAKES: about 300 ml/10 fl oz	**PREP TIME:** 5 mins	**COOK TIME:** 15 mins

THIS CREAMY NACHO SAUCE GETS ITS HEAT FROM MUSTARD POWDER, HOT SAUCE AND FINELY CHOPPED CHILLIES. YOU CAN TOP TORTILLA CHIPS WITH THE SAUCE OR ALTERNATIVELY MIX IT WITH COOKED PASTA OR ADD IT TO JACKET POTATOES.

INGREDIENTS

125 g/4½ oz mature Cheddar cheese, coarsely grated

3 tbsp cornflour

1 tbsp mustard powder

250 ml/9 fl oz milk

2 tbsp cream cheese

2 tsp sriracha or other hot chilli sauce

2 red or green jalapeño chillies, finely chopped

salt and pepper (optional)

1. Mix together the Cheddar cheese, cornflour and mustard powder in a heatproof bowl, then set aside.

2. Put the milk into a saucepan and bring just to the boil. Stir 4 tablespoons of the hot milk into the cheese mixture, stirring until well blended. Add the cheese mixture to the milk, whisking vigorously.

3. Bring the mixture back just to the boil, then reduce the heat and simmer, whisking frequently, for 5 minutes, until the sauce is smooth and has reduced. Remove the pan from the heat and stir in the cream cheese and chilli sauce. Season with salt and pepper, if using, then stir in the chillies.

4. The sauce can be used immediately, or left to cool completely and stored in an airtight container in the refrigerator for up to 3 days. To serve, reheat gently without boiling.

TIP

DO NOT ADD THE CORNFLOUR OR MUSTARD POWDER DIRECTLY TO THE HOT MILK OR LUMPS WILL FORM. WHISK TO ENSURE A SMOOTH MIXTURE.

DANGEROUS
ADOBO SAUCE

| **MAKES:** about 300 ml/10 fl oz | **PREP TIME:** 10 mins | **COOK TIME:** 1½–1¾ hrs |

CHIPOTLE CHILLIES ARE DRIED JALAPEÑO CHILLIES, WHICH ARE AVAILABLE IN TWO FORMS, MORITA OR MECO. MECO CHIPOTLES GIVE A SMOKIER FLAVOUR THAT WORKS WELL WITH SLOW-COOKED MEAT DISHES.

INGREDIENTS

4 tbsp tomato purée
600 ml/1 pint water
6 tbsp white wine vinegar
12 dried chipotle chillies, stems removed
4 garlic cloves, crushed
½ red onion, very finely chopped
2 tbsp soft light brown sugar
1 tbsp ground cumin
1 tbsp dried Mexican oregano or dried thyme
2 tsp hot smoked paprika
2 tsp cayenne pepper
½ tsp salt
pepper (optional)

1. Dissolve the tomato purée in the water and vinegar in a deep pan. Stir in the other ingredients and season with pepper, if using. Cover and bring to the boil.

2. Uncover, reduce the heat to very low and simmer for 1¼–1½ hours, or until the chillies are very soft and the sauce thickens.

3. Transfer the sauce to a blender or food processor and purée. Strain the sauce through a sieve into a bowl, rubbing backwards and forwards with a wooden spoon and scraping the base of the sieve to produce as much purée as possible. Set aside to cool completely.

4. The sauce can be used immediately, or stored in an airtight container in the refrigerator for up to 3 weeks.

MEATBALLS IN
ADOBO SAUCE

SERVES: 4	PREP TIME: 20 mins	COOK TIME: 30–35 mins

WHEN YOU'RE EXPECTING CHILLI LOVERS FOR DINNER, THIS IS A GREAT QUICK AND EASY DISH TO SERVE. THE SAUCE IS SPICY HOT AND ANY LEFTOVERS MAKE A GREAT TACO FILLING.

INGREDIENTS

40 g/1½ oz dried breadcrumbs

3–4 tbsp milk

3 tbsp plain flour, for dusting

250 g/9 oz lean beef mince

250 g/9 oz lean pork mince

4 large garlic cloves, finely chopped

2 eggs, beaten

3 tbsp finely chopped fresh parsley or coriander

1 tsp ground cinnamon

1 tsp sweet paprika

4 tbsp sunflower oil, for frying, plus extra if needed

300 ml/10 fl oz Dangerous Adobo Sauce (see previous page)

125 g/4½ oz mozzarella cheese, roughly chopped

4 tbsp coarsely grated Cheddar cheese

salt and pepper (optional)

1. Combine the breadcrumbs and milk in a bowl and leave to soak for 10 minutes. Put the flour on a plate and set aside. Preheat the oven to 200°C/400°F/Gas Mark 6.

2. Combine the beef, pork, garlic, eggs, parsley, cinnamon and paprika with the breadcrumb mixture in a large bowl. Season to taste with salt and pepper, if using, and stir to combine.

3. Using wet hands, shape the mixture into 24 equal-sized balls. Heat the oil in a large frying pan over a medium heat. Working in batches, lightly roll the meatballs in the flour, shaking off the excess. Add the meatballs to the pan and fry, turning, until brown all over, then transfer to a baking dish.

4. Pour the Adobo Sauce over the meatballs in the dish, then sprinkle over the mozzarella cheese and Cheddar cheese. Bake in the preheated oven for 15–20 minutes, or until the meatballs are cooked through, the sauce is hot and the cheese is melting.

5. Meanwhile, preheat the grill to high. Place the dish under the grill and brown for 2–3 minutes.

VEGETABLE MAINS & SIDES

This chapter focuses on vegetable dishes – be prepared as they are charged with smoky spices and fiery chillies. Aubergines, courgettes, butternut squash and celeriac are all given the treatment. Our selection ranges from Celeriac, Fennel & Peach Slaw and Gratin of Green Chillies to Sweet Potato & Halloumi Burgers and Smokey Barbecue Beans.

AUBERGINES
STUFFED WITH BULGAR WHEAT

| SERVES: 4 | PREP TIME: 35 mins | COOK TIME: 55 mins |

A GOOD SOURCE OF VITAMINS, MINERALS AND FIBRE, PURPLE-SKINNED AUBERGINES WORK WELL WITH SPICES IN THIS WHOLESOME DISH. FIBRE-RICH BULGAR WHEAT PROVIDES THE BASE FOR THE HERBY-VEGETABLE STUFFING.

INGREDIENTS

1 tsp ground cumin
1 tsp ground coriander
1 tsp paprika
1 tsp chilli flakes
2 tbsp olive oil
2 aubergines, cut in half lengthways
1 red onion, roughly chopped
2 garlic cloves, chopped
150 g/5½ oz fine bulgar wheat
200 ml/7 fl oz vegetable stock
3 tbsp roughly chopped fresh coriander
3 tbsp roughly chopped fresh mint
125 g/4½ oz feta cheese, crumbled
30 g/1 oz flaked almonds, toasted
1½ tbsp lemon juice
2 tsp pomegranate molasses
salt and pepper (optional)
1 tbsp chopped fresh mint, to garnish
1 tsp pomegranate molasses, to garnish
125 g/4½ oz Greek-style natural yogurt, to garnish
4 tbsp pomegranate seeds, to garnish

1. Preheat the oven to 180°C/350°F/Gas Mark 4. Mix the cumin, ground coriander, paprika, chilli flakes and 1½ tablespoons of olive oil in a small bowl. Use a sharp knife to slice the aubergine flesh in a diagonal, criss-cross pattern, without piercing the skin. Drizzle the cumin mixture over the aubergines, allowing it to sink in to the cuts. Place the aubergine halves on a baking sheet and roast in the oven for 35 minutes.

2. Meanwhile, heat the remaining half a tablespoon of olive oil in a large frying pan over a medium heat. Add the onion and garlic and fry for 3–4 minutes, or until softened. Reduce the heat, add the bulgar wheat and stir well. Reduce the heat to low, pour over the vegetable stock and stir until the liquid has been absorbed. Remove the mixture from the pan and transfer to a large bowl.

3. Remove the aubergines from the oven and leave to rest for 10 minutes. Leave the oven on. Using a dessertspoon, scoop out the centre of the aubergine, leaving a clear edge to support the filling.

4. Add the aubergine flesh to the bulgar mixture. Stir in the fresh coriander, mint, feta, almonds, lemon juice and pomegranate molasses. Stir well and season with salt and pepper, if using.

5. Divide the stuffing between the aubergines and return to the oven for 15 minutes. Serve immediately, garnished with the fresh mint, molasses, yogurt and pomegranate seeds.

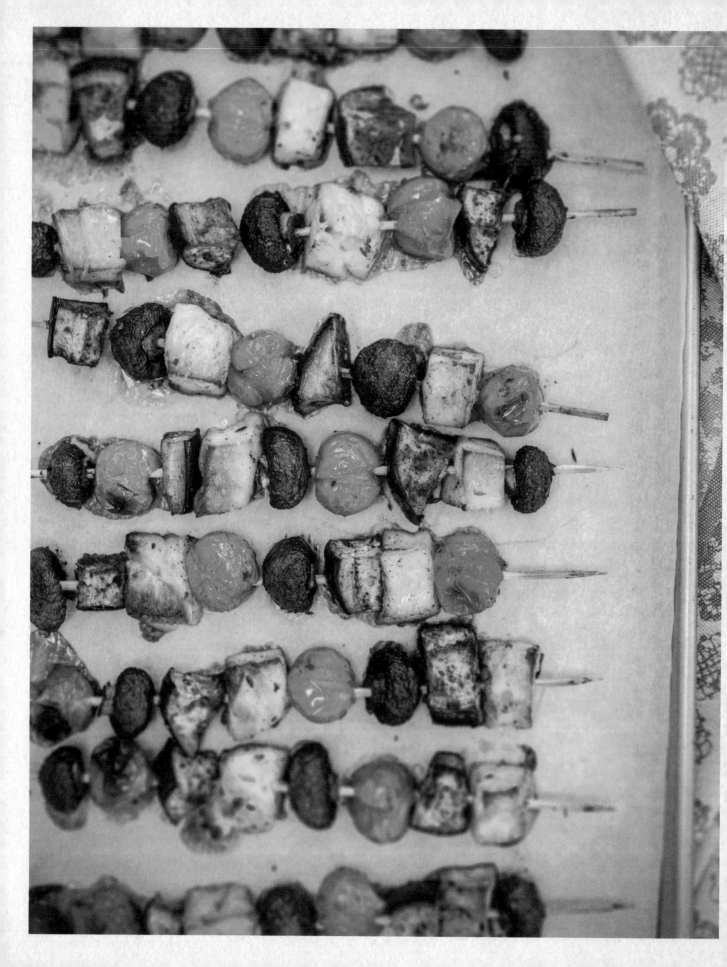

SPICED VEGETABLE & HALLOUMI SKEWERS

SERVES: 8	PREP TIME: 25 mins	COOK TIME: 30 minutes

THESE SPICED SKEWERS MAKE A GREAT VEGETARIAN OPTION FOR BARBECUES AND, SIMPLE TO MAKE, THEY ARE PERFECT FOR A CROWD. YOU WILL NEED 16 WOODEN SKEWERS FOR THIS RECIPE.

INGREDIENTS

250 g/9 oz chestnut mushrooms, halved or quartered depending on size

250 g/9 oz halloumi cheese, cut into 15-mm/⅝-inch chunks

1 large aubergine, cut into 2-cm/¾-inch chunks

450 g/1 lb cherry tomatoes

1 tbsp ras el hanout

1 tsp sea salt flakes

3 tbsp olive oil

pinch of sea salt flakes

1. Preheat the oven to 180°C/350°F/Gas Mark 4. Soak 16 wooden skewers in water for 20 minutes, then drain well.

2. Put the mushrooms, halloumi, aubergine and cherry tomatoes in a large bowl and toss well. Add the ras el hanout, 1 teaspoon of salt and the oil and toss again.

3. Thread the vegetables and halloumi onto the skewers in any combination, then place them on two large baking trays. Roast for 30 minutes, or until the vegetables are tender. Sprinkle with a large pinch of salt and serve two skewers per person.

TIP

IF YOU WISH, ASSEMBLE THE SKEWERS IN ADVANCE AND LET THEM MARINATE FOR A FEW HOURS IN THE FRIDGE BEFORE COOKING.

RED KIDNEY BEAN
CURRY

| SERVES: 4 | PREP TIME: 20 mins | COOK TIME: 30–35 mins |

HIGH IN FIBRE, THIS DELICIOUS NORTHERN INDIAN DISH OF SPICED RED KIDNEY BEANS IS BEST SERVED WITH RICE AND WARMED FLATBREADS. IT CAN EASILY BE MADE A DAY AHEAD – SIMPLY REHEAT IT AND SERVE WITH THE YOGURT.

INGREDIENTS

2 tbsp vegetable or groundnut oil

2 tsp cumin seeds

2 onions, finely chopped

2 tsp grated fresh ginger

6 garlic cloves, crushed

2 fresh green chillies, finely chopped

2 large tomatoes, roughly chopped

2 tsp ground coriander

1 tsp ground cumin

¼ tsp ground turmeric

1 tsp garam masala

800 g/1 lb 12 oz canned red kidney beans, drained and rinsed

1 tsp palm sugar

500 ml/17 fl oz warm water

1 tsp salt

4 tbsp finely chopped fresh coriander, to garnish

2 tbsp natural yogurt, to serve

1. Heat the oil in a large saucepan and add the cumin seeds. When they stop crackling, add the onions and fry until soft.

2. Add the ginger and garlic and fry for 2 minutes. Add the chillies, tomatoes, ground coriander, cumin, turmeric and garam masala and stir-fry for 12–15 minutes.

3. Add the red kidney beans, palm sugar, water and salt and cook for 10–12 minutes, or until the beans are soft.

4. Remove from the heat and transfer to a serving dish. Garnish with the chopped coriander and serve with the yogurt.

TIP

CANNED BEANS ARE USED IN THIS RECIPE FOR SPEED. IF USING DRIED BEANS, COOK ACCORDING TO THE PACKET INSTRUCTIONS BEFORE USING.

BENGALI
VEGETABLE CURRY

| SERVES: 4 | PREP TIME: 30 mins, plus standing | COOK TIME: 30–35 mins |

THIS TRADITIONAL BENGALI VEGETABLE CURRY USES A MIXTURE OF CHOPPED VEGETABLES AND IS COOKED WITH A MUSTARD SEED AND WHITE POPPY SEED PASTE. PANCH PHORAN IS A BENGALI SPICE MIXTURE MADE OF FENUGREEK SEEDS, FENNEL SEEDS, MUSTARD SEEDS, NIGELLA SEEDS AND CUMIN SEEDS.

INGREDIENTS

6 tbsp white poppy seeds (khus khus)

3 tbsp black mustard seeds

2 tsp grated fresh ginger

4 tbsp vegetable or groundnut oil

2 fresh green chillies, split lengthways

1 tbsp panch phoran

200 g/7 oz fresh bitter gourd (kerala), cut into 1.5-cm/⁵/₈-inch cubes

2 potatoes, peeled and cut into 1.5-cm/⁵/₈-inch cubes

1 aubergine, cut into 1.5-cm/⁵/₈-inch cubes

1 courgette, cut into 1.5-cm/⁵/₈-inch cubes

1 carrot, cut into 1.5-cm/⁵/₈-inch cubes

1 tomato, finely chopped

100 g/3½ oz fresh or frozen peas

400 ml/14 fl oz cold water

¼ tsp ground turmeric

2 tsp salt

1 tsp palm sugar

125 ml/4 fl oz milk

1. Soak the white poppy seeds and 2 tablespoons of the mustard seeds in warm water for 1 hour. Drain and blend with the ginger to make a paste.

2. Heat the oil in a large frying pan and add the remaining mustard seeds and the chillies. When the mustard seeds start to pop, add the panch phoran and all the vegetables. Add half the water and stir to mix well, then cover tightly and cook, stirring frequently, over a medium heat for 10–12 minutes.

3. Add half the white poppy seed and mustard seed paste, the turmeric and salt. Add the remaining water and cook, stirring frequently, over a low-medium heat for a further 10–15 minutes.

4. Add the remaining white poppy seed and mustard seed paste, the palm sugar and milk and cook for a further 5 minutes, or until the vegetables are tender. Serve hot.

SPICY COUSCOUS WITH NUTS, DATES & APRICOTS

SERVES: 4	PREP TIME: 15 mins	COOK TIME: 15 mins

COUSCOUS COMBINED WITH DRIED FRUIT AND NUTS IS DELICIOUS SERVED WITH GRILLED MEATS AND SPICY TAGINES. TRADITIONALLY A FRUITY COUSCOUS WOULD ALSO BE DUSTED WITH CINNAMON AND SERVED ON ITS OWN, OFTEN AS A PALATE CLEANSER.

INGREDIENTS

350 g/12 oz couscous

400 ml/14 fl oz boiling water

½ tsp sea salt flakes

2 tbsp olive oil

1–2 tbsp clarified butter

large pinch of saffron threads

115 g/4 oz blanched almonds

115 g/4 oz unsalted pistachio nuts

1–2 tsp ras el hanout

115 g/4 oz dates, thinly sliced

115 g/4 oz ready-to-eat dried apricots, thinly sliced

2 tsp ground cinnamon, to garnish

1. Tip the couscous into a shallow heatproof bowl. Put the boiling water in a jug, stir in the salt, then pour it over the couscous, cover and leave for 10 minutes.

2. Drizzle the oil over the couscous. Using your fingers, rub it into the grains to break up the lumps.

3. Heat the butter in a heavy-based frying pan over a medium heat. Add the saffron, almonds and pistachio nuts and cook for 1–2 minutes, or until the nuts begin to brown and emit a nutty aroma, stirring occasionally. Stir in the ras el hanout, toss in the dates and dried apricots and cook, stirring, for 2 minutes. Fluff up the couscous using a fork, then tip it into the pan, mix well and heat through. Remove from the heat.

4. Pile the couscous onto a serving plate in a mound. Rub the cinnamon through your fingers to create vertical lines from the top of the mound to the base, like the spokes of a wheel. Serve immediately.

GRATIN OF
GREEN CHILLIES
WITH CREAM & CHEESE

SERVES: 4–6	PREP TIME: 20–25 mins, plus standing	COOK TIME: 25 mins

THE UTTERLY DELICIOUS COMBINATION OF PEPPERY, LEMONY CHILLIES AND SWEET, RICH CREAM OFFERS THE PERFECT BALANCE OF TEXTURE AND FLAVOUR.

INGREDIENTS

750 g/1 lb 10 oz thin-fleshed, mild green chillies, preferably Anaheim

275 ml/9 fl oz single cream

275 ml/9 fl oz double cream

250 g/9 oz feta-type crumbly salty white cheese, crumbled

salt and pepper (optional)

soft cornmeal tortillas, to serve

1. Wipe the chillies, but don't remove the stalks or seeds. Using tongs, hold the chillies over a gas flame, or cook under a preheated grill or oven on the highest setting, until the skins are black and blistered in places. Transfer to a polythene or paper bag and leave to stand for 10 minutes to loosen the skins. Remove the skins. Slice the flesh into ribbons and arrange in a gratin dish.

2. Meanwhile, heat all the cream in a small saucepan and remove it as soon as it reaches boiling point. Pour over the chilli ribbons and sprinkle with the cheese. Season with a little salt and pepper – not too much, as the cheese is already salty and one or two of the chillies may be fiery.

3. Preheat the grill to very high. Cook the chillies for 8–10 minutes, or until brown and bubbling. Meanwhile, wrap the tortillas in foil and warm through in a preheated low oven for 5 minutes. Serve the gratin piping hot, with the warmed tortillas for mopping up.

SWEET POTATO & HALLOUMI BURGERS

| MAKES: 4–6 | PREP TIME: 10–12 mins, plus chilling | COOK TIME: 45–50 mins |

THERE ARE LOTS OF INTERESTING TEXTURES AND FLAVOURS VYING FOR YOUR ATTENTION IN THESE TASTY VEGETARIAN BURGERS.

INGREDIENTS

salt for cooking the sweet potatoes

450 g/1 lb sweet potatoes, cut into chunks

175 g/6 oz broccoli florets

2–3 garlic cloves, crushed

1 red onion, finely chopped or grated

1½–2 fresh red jalapeño chillies, deseeded and finely chopped

175 g/6 oz halloumi cheese, grated

2 tbsp wholemeal flour

2–3 tbsp sunflower oil

450 g/1 lb onions, sliced

1 tbsp chopped fresh coriander

salt and pepper (optional)

1. Bring a saucepan of lightly salted water to the boil, add the sweet potatoes, bring back to the boil and cook for 15–20 minutes, or until tender. Drain and mash. Bring a separate small saucepan of lightly salted water to the boil, add the broccoli, bring back to the boil and cook for 3 minutes, then drain and plunge into cold water. Drain again, then add to the mashed sweet potato.

2. Stir in the garlic, red onion, chillies, cheese, and salt and pepper to taste, if using. Mix well and shape into 4–6 equal-sized patties, then coat in the flour. Cover and leave to chill in the refrigerator for at least 1 hour.

3. Heat 1½ tablespoons of the oil in a heavy-based frying pan. Add the onions and fry over a medium heat for 12–15 minutes, or until soft. Stir in the coriander and reserve.

4. Preheat the barbecue. Brush the patties with the remaining oil and cook over a medium heat for 5–6 minutes on each side, or until cooked through.

5. Top the burgers with the reserved fried onions and coriander and serve immediately.

VEGETABLE CHILLI

| SERVES: 4 | PREP TIME: 35 mins | COOK TIME: 1 hr 20 mins |

THIS DELICIOUS, SPICY VEGETARIAN CHILLI IS FULL OF VEGETABLES, BEANS, AND WONDERFUL FLAVOURS. YOU CAN INCREASE THE AMOUNT OF CHILLI POWDER AND CUMIN IF YOU WANT TO INCREASE THE HEAT FACTOR.

INGREDIENTS

1 aubergine, cut into 2.5-cm/1-inch slices

2 tbsp olive oil

1 large red onion, finely chopped

2 red or yellow peppers, deseeded and finely chopped

3–4 garlic cloves, finely chopped

800 g/1 lb 12 oz canned chopped tomatoes

1 tbsp mild chilli powder

½ tsp ground cumin

½ tsp dried oregano

2 small courgettes, quartered lengthways and sliced

400 g/14 oz canned kidney beans, drained and rinsed

450 ml/15 fl oz water

1 tbsp tomato purée

6 spring onions, finely chopped

115 g/4 oz Cheddar cheese, grated, for sprinkling

salt and pepper (optional)

1. Brush the aubergine slices on one side with oil. Heat half the remaining oil in a large, heavy-based frying pan over a medium–high heat. Add the aubergine slices oiled side up and cook for 5–6 minutes, or until brown on one side. Turn the slices over, cook on the other side until brown and transfer to a plate. Cut into bite-sized pieces.

2. Heat the remaining oil in a large saucepan over a medium heat. Add the onion and red peppers and cook, stirring occasionally, for 3–4 minutes, or until the onion is soft but not brown.

3. Add the garlic and cook for a further 2–3 minutes, or until the onion is beginning to colour.

4. Add the tomatoes, chilli powder, cumin and oregano. Season with salt and pepper, if using. Bring just to the boil, reduce the heat, cover and simmer gently for 15 minutes.

5. Add the courgettes, aubergine pieces and beans. Stir in the water and the tomato purée. Bring back to the boil, then cover and continue simmering for 45 minutes, or until the vegetables are tender. Add salt and pepper, if using. Ladle into serving bowls, top with the spring onions and sprinkle over the cheese. Serve.

CHILLI SAUCES AROUND THE WORLD

Although chillies originated in South and Central America, they are now grown in just about every part of the world – and are a key part of the many hot and spicy flavours we associate with particular regions.

South America

The home of the chilli produces a traditionally mild cuisine – so the addition of a sauce is often needed to add a little fire, although even the hot sauces tend to focus on flavour rather than heat. The most popular remains adobo sauce, made from chillies such as chipotle, with Mexican oregano, onions and tomatoes; but all amateur chefs will have their own recipe, often using chipotle or jalapeño chillies.

USA

US hot sauces are made with chillies, vinegar and salt – but often with the addition of fruits and vegetables as diverse as raspberries, mangoes, tomatoes and carrots to mellow out the flavour or add a thick edge to the sauce. The most popular chillies used in US sauces are jalapeño, chipotle, habañero and cayenne, and results range from very mild barbecue sauces to the spicy hot pepper sauce.

Caribbean

Sauces made from chillies feature heavily in Caribbean cuisine and, like their US cousins, most are made with the addition of fruit and vegetables to temper the flavour. However, as most Caribbean sauces feature habañero and Scotch bonnet chillies, the results still tend to be far hotter! Home-made sauces are very common too, with flavours as strong as onions and garlic often added for extra piquancy.

Europe

Believe it or not, two of the hottest chilli sauces in the world originate from the UK! Made from the naga viper and infinity chillies, they remain a specialized taste. However, the Portuguese peri-peri sauce, made from crushed peri-peri chillies with lime, citrus peel, garlic and various herbs, remains popular across the continent.

Middle East

The ancients of this region believed that chillies held near-magical healing powers, and so much of the traditional cuisine features sauces with chillies as ingredients. The most popular remains harissa – made from fresh and dried hot chillies blended into a thick paste with garlic, olive oil and spices such as caraway seeds. Other examples are *shatta*, used in Levantine cuisine, made with chillies and olive oil, and *skhug* from Yemen and Israel.

Asia

Chilli sauces are used widely in Asia. Often made with the addition of beans, many sauces are made as a thick paste, which can be added to curries, as a dipping sauce or for stir-frying. India is one of the largest chilli producers and they define the experience of many of the dishes (see jwala chillies, opposite, left). Specific Asian sauces include the Chinese Lao Gan Ma combining chillies with soybean paste, and the Korean gochujang, made with chilli, glutinous rice, fermented soybeans and salt. Thailand is known for its sriracha sauce, as used in Salmon Satay with Sriracha Sauce (opposite, right), as well as its spicy dipping sauces (nam chim) and fish sauces (nam pla). Sambal is a chilli sauce from Indonesia, Malaysia and Sri Lanka that has developed an international appeal.

BUTTERNUT SQUASH
LINGUINE WITH
ARRABBIATA SAUCE

SERVES: 2	PREP TIME: 15 mins	COOK TIME: 20 mins

WE ALL LOVE PASTA, BUT OCCASIONALLY IT'S GREAT TO TRY SOMETHING DIFFERENT – VEGETABLES PREPARED SO THEY LOOK VERY MUCH LIKE SPAGHETTI TASTE GREAT, BUT ARE LOW IN CARBS!

INGREDIENTS

1 butternut squash
8 sprays cooking oil spray
2 tbsp chopped fresh flat-leaf parsley, to garnish

ARRABBIATA SAUCE

1 tbsp olive oil
1 onion, chopped
2 garlic cloves, crushed
1 red chilli, deseeded and finely chopped
3 tbsp red wine
1 tsp sugar
1 tsp chilli flakes
2 tsp red pesto
200 g/7 oz canned chopped tomatoes
4 anchovy fillets from a jar, drained
8 black olives, stoned and roughly chopped
1 tsp dried Italian seasoning
½ tsp salt
½ tsp pepper

1. Cut the bulbous end off the squash and set aside for another recipe. Cut the stalk off the squash and discard. Peel the remaining squash. If you are using a spiralizer, cut the squash into two chunks and put each chunk through the spiralizer. If you are using a julienne peeler, set the squash on a stable work surface and slice off julienne strips.

2. To make the arrabbiata sauce, place a large saucepan over a medium-low heat and add the oil. Add the onion and fry for 8 minutes, or until soft and transparent. Add the garlic and chilli and stir for 1 minute. Add the wine, sugar, chilli flakes, pesto, tomatoes, anchovies, olives, Italian seasoning, salt and pepper and simmer for 20 minutes.

3. Meanwhile, preheat the oven to 190°C/375°F/Gas Mark 5. Put the squash spaghetti on a large baking tray and spray with the cooking oil spray. Bake in the preheated oven for 6 minutes, and then turn the spaghetti over using tongs. Bake for a further 4 minutes, or until the strands are just tender with the occasional tinge of gold.

4. Transfer the spaghetti to two warmed serving plates. Spoon the arrabbiata sauce over the spaghetti, garnish with the parsley and serve immediately.

CELERIAC, FENNEL & PEACH SLAW

SERVES: 4	PREP TIME: 10 mins	COOK TIME: none

A GOOD SLAW, THIS ONE SPICED UP WITH SRIRACHA CHILLI SAUCE, CAN BE USED IN SO MANY WAYS – AS A QUICK SNACK, AS A SANDWICH OR WRAP COMPONENT OR SERVED WITH COLD MEAT AND A CRISPY SALAD.

INGREDIENTS

4 tbsp mayonnaise
1 tsp sriracha chilli sauce
1 tsp horseradish sauce
zest and juice of 1 lemon
½ tsp pepper
2 ripe peaches, stoned and sliced
200 g/7 oz celeriac, cut into matchsticks
1 fennel bulb, sliced
1 small red onion, sliced

1. In a large bowl, whisk together the mayonnaise, chilli sauce, horseradish sauce, lemon zest and juice, and pepper.

2. Add the peaches, celeriac, fennel and onion to the bowl.

3. Mix well to combine thoroughly, then serve immediately.

TIP

THIS SLAW WILL WORK WELL WITH ANY STONE FRUIT AND IS GREAT SERVED WITH PORK, CHICKEN OR FISH.

SMOKEY BBQ
BEANS

SERVES: 4	PREP TIME: 10 mins	COOK TIME: 30 mins

THE CANNELLINI BEANS IN THIS RECIPE ARE INFUSED WITH DEEP-SEATED, SMOKEY FLAVOURS, WITH THE FINAL DISH COMBINING TENDER, CREAMY BEANS WITH AN ADDICTIVE BARBECUE FLAVOUR.

INGREDIENTS

4 tbsp olive oil

1 large onion, chopped

2 garlic cloves, chopped

2 celery sticks, chopped

1 large carrot, chopped

1 tsp fennel seeds

2 tsp dried oregano

2 tsp smoked paprika

1 tbsp chipotle chilli paste

1 tbsp black treacle

450 ml/15 fl oz passata

400 g/14 oz canned cannellini beans, drained and rinsed

salt and pepper (optional)

1. Heat the oil in a large saucepan over a medium heat. Add the onion, garlic, celery and carrot and sweat with a lid on for 15 minutes, or until translucent and soft.

2. Add the fennel seeds, oregano, paprika, chilli paste and treacle. Cook for 5 minutes, until the sugars start to caramelize.

3. Add the passata and beans and cook for a further 10 minutes.

4. Season with salt and pepper, if using, and serve.

TIP

FOR THE CARNIVORE IN YOUR LIFE, TRY ADDING CHOPPED SMOKED BACON OR CHORIZO TO THE BEANS.

SPICED
AUBERGINE MASH

| SERVES: 4 | PREP TIME: 15–20 mins | COOK TIME: 45–55 mins |

THIS VERSION OF BAINGAN KA BHARTA HAS ITS ORIGINS IN THE PUNJAB. BHARTAS ARE LARGELY NORTH INDIAN IN ORIGIN AND CAN BE MADE FROM ALL SORTS OF VEGETABLES.

INGREDIENTS

4 large aubergines
2 tbsp vegetable or groundnut oil
55 g/2 oz butter
2 onions, finely chopped
2 tsp grated fresh ginger
4 garlic cloves, crushed
2 fresh green chillies, finely sliced
3 tomatoes, finely chopped
2 tsp salt
1 tsp chilli powder
1 tsp smoked paprika
2 tsp ground coriander
1 tsp ground cumin
1 tsp ground turmeric
½ tsp garam masala
6 tbsp finely chopped fresh coriander

1. Prick the aubergines all over with a fork and roast them over an open flame (if you have a gas hob) or under a medium-hot grill, turning them from time to time, for 20–25 minutes, until the skin blackens and chars. To check if the aubergines are cooked, press the back of a spoon into the skin – if it enters the aubergine like soft butter, it is done. Leave to cool.

2. When the aubergines are cool enough to handle, remove the skins and roughly mash the pulp. Set aside.

3. Heat the oil and butter in a large, non-stick frying pan and add the onions. Sauté for 5–6 minutes, until soft. Add the ginger, garlic and chillies and stir-fry for 1–2 minutes.

4. Stir in the tomatoes and salt and cook for 12–15 minutes. Add the chilli powder, paprika, ground coriander, cumin and turmeric.

5. Stir in the reserved aubergine flesh and cook for about 3–4 minutes. Stir in the garam masala and fresh coriander. Serve immediately.

THAI RED CHIPS

SERVES: 4	PREP TIME: 15 mins	COOK TIME: 30 mins

THESE UNUSUAL OVEN-BAKED CHIPS HIT ALL THE RIGHT TASTE BUDS – SWEET, SPICY, TANGY, SALTY AND ALL-ROUND DELICIOUS.

INGREDIENTS

3 tbsp vegetable oil
2 tbsp soft light brown sugar
2 tbsp Thai fish sauce
2 tbsp lime juice
1 tbsp Thai red curry paste
½ tsp cayenne pepper
900 g/2 lb potatoes

CORIANDER KETCHUP

1 garlic clove
15 g/½ oz fresh coriander
225 ml/8 fl oz tomato ketchup
2 tbsp lime juice

1. Preheat the oven to 230°C/450°F/Gas Mark 8. Grease a large baking sheet with 1 tbsp of the oil.

2. Put the remaining oil, sugar, fish sauce, lime juice, curry paste and cayenne pepper into a mixing bowl and stir together until well combined.

3. Peel the potatoes, if desired, and cut them into 5 x 5-mm/ ¼ x ¼-inch sticks. Add them to the mixture in the bowl and toss to coat. Leave to stand for about 5 minutes, then, using a slotted spoon, transfer the potatoes to the prepared baking sheet, allowing the excess marinade to run off into the bowl. Spread the potatoes in a single layer. Bake in the preheated oven for 25–30 minutes, turning after about 15 minutes, until brown and crisp.

4. Meanwhile, to make the ketchup, chop the garlic and coriander in a food processor. Add the ketchup and lime juice and process until well combined. Transfer to a serving bowl.

5. Serve the chips hot with the ketchup for dipping.

MEAT & POULTRY MAINS

When it's a sizzling, spice-packed meaty main that's
needed, these dishes won't disappoint. Choose from
chicken, turkey, beef, pork or lamb, and impress your
family and friends with Goan Spiced Chicken; Hot
Sesame Beef; Turkey Stir-Fry with Spiced Coffee Glaze;
Pork with Chillies, Vinegar & Garlic; or treat yourself to
a Colossal Lamb Kebab with Hot Chilli Sauce.

GOAN
SPICED CHICKEN

| SERVES: 4 | PREP TIME: 20 mins | COOK TIME: 35–40 mins |

THIS CLASSIC, SPICY CHICKEN DISH FROM THE SHORES OF GOA IS A LOCAL FAVOURITE. MADE FROM A BLEND OF COCONUT MILK, RED CHILLIES AND AROMATIC SPICES, IT IS BEST SERVED WITH STEAMED RICE AND MANGO CHUTNEY.

INGREDIENTS

6 black peppercorns
3 cloves
2 tsp fennel seeds
4 dried red chillies
1 tsp cardamom seeds
2 tsp white poppy seeds
2 cinnamon sticks
2 tsp salt
1 tsp ground turmeric
1 tsp ground cumin
1 tsp ground coriander
4 tbsp vegetable or groundnut oil
1 onion, very finely chopped
3 garlic cloves, crushed
600 g/1 lb 5 oz skinless, boneless chicken thighs, cut into bite-sized pieces
400 ml/14 fl oz coconut milk
300 ml/10 fl oz cold water
1 tsp tamarind paste

1. Place a large, non-stick frying pan over a medium heat and add the peppercorns, cloves, fennel seeds, dried red chillies, cardamom seeds, white poppy seeds and cinnamon sticks. Dry-fry for 1–2 minutes, then remove from the heat and allow to cool.

2. Place the cooled whole spices into a spice grinder with the salt, turmeric, cumin and ground coriander. Process until ground to a fairly fine powder.

3. Heat the oil in a large saucepan, add the onion and garlic and cook over a medium heat for 2–3 minutes. Increase the heat to high, add the chicken and stir-fry for 5–6 minutes, or until sealed.

4. Tip in the spice mixture and stir-fry for 1–2 minutes, then add the coconut milk and water. Bring to the boil, then reduce the heat to low–medium and simmer gently for 15–20 minutes. Stir in the tamarind paste and cook for a further 2–3 minutes, or until the chicken is cooked through and tender. Serve immediately.

SPICY BEEF BURGERS
WITH GUACAMOLE & WEDGES

SERVES: 4	PREP TIME: 1 hr	COOK TIME: 45 mins

A GOOD BEEF BURGER IS HARD TO BEAT, AND IF YOU MAKE YOUR OWN YOU'LL KNOW WHAT IS IN IT AND WHERE THE MEAT HAS COME FROM.

INGREDIENTS

500 g/1 lb 2 oz rump steak, visible fat removed, diced

½ tsp chilli powder

2 tsp cumin seeds, roughly crushed

1 tbsp fresh thyme leaves

700 g/1 lb 9 oz baking potatoes, unpeeled, scrubbed and cut into wedges

3 tbsp virgin olive oil

1 tsp paprika

sea salt and pepper (optional)

GUACAMOLE

1 large avocado, stoned and peeled

juice of 1 lime

2 spring onions, finely chopped

TO SERVE

4 spelt rolls, halved

1 Romaine lettuce heart, shredded

handful of rocket leaves

2 large tomatoes, sliced

1. Preheat the oven to 200°C/400°F/Gas Mark 6. With the motor running on a food processor, drop in a few pieces of steak at a time, until it has all been roughly chopped. Alternatively, press the pieces through a mincer on the coarse setting.

2. Put the chilli powder, half the cumin seeds, half the thyme and a little salt and pepper, if using, in a bowl and mix well. Rub this into the steak, then shape the mixture into four burgers. Cover and chill in the refrigerator for 15 minutes.

3. Bring a saucepan of water to the boil, add the wedges and cook for 4–5 minutes. Drain well and tip into a roasting tin. Drizzle the wedges with 2 tablespoons of oil, then turn them until they are well coated. Sprinkle with the paprika, the remaining cumin and thyme and a little salt and pepper, if using. Bake, turning once, for 25–30 minutes, or until golden brown.

4. For the guacamole, put the avocado in a shallow bowl and mash with a fork. Add the lime juice and spring onions, season with a little salt and pepper, if using, and mix well.

5. Preheat the grill to medium-high. Brush the burgers with a little of the remaining oil, then cook, turning halfway through, for 8–10 minutes, or a little less for those who like their burgers pink in the middle. Leave to stand for a few minutes. Meanwhile, toast the rolls, then top the bases with lettuce, rocket and tomatoes, the hot burgers, and a spoonful of guacamole and the roll lids. Serve with the wedges.

TURKEY STIR-FRY
WITH SPICED COFFEE GLAZE

SERVES: 4	PREP TIME: 25 mins, plus marinating	COOK TIME: 15 mins

THIS TEMPTING, FLAVOURSOME STIR-FRY REQUIRES ONLY FIFTEEN MINUTES COOKING AND IT WILL UNDOUBTEDLY SPICE UP YOUR DAY.

INGREDIENTS

400 g/14 oz turkey breast fillet, sliced into thin strips

1 tsp finely grated fresh ginger

2 garlic cloves, crushed

1 tsp five-spice paste

4 tsp sesame oil

4 tbsp strong black coffee, cooled

4 tbsp teriyaki sauce

2 tbsp clear honey

2 tbsp rice wine vinegar

2 tsp cornflour

6 spring onions, trimmed and sliced

1 red pepper, deseeded and thinly sliced

1 yellow pepper, deseeded and thinly sliced

salt and pepper (optional)

500 g/1 lb 2 oz boiled egg noodles, to serve

1. Place the turkey in a shallow, non-metallic bowl and add the ginger, garlic, five-spice paste and half the oil. Stir well, then cover and leave to marinate at room temperature for 1 hour.

2. Mix together the coffee, teriyaki sauce, honey, vinegar and cornflour in a jug. Cover and set aside.

3. Heat the remaining oil in a large wok until almost smoking. Remove the turkey from the marinade, add to the wok and stir-fry over a high heat for 3–4 minutes, until brown. Add the spring onions, red pepper and yellow pepper and stir-fry for a further 1–2 minutes.

4. Pour in the coffee mixture and continue stir-frying for 1–2 minutes, until the sauce has thickened and coated the turkey and vegetables. Serve with the noodles.

HOT SESAME BEEF

SERVES: 4	PREP TIME: 20 mins	COOK TIME: 10 mins

THIS SESAME BEEF IS BEAUTIFULLY SUCCULENT AND STICKY, WITH THE BEEF AND VEGETABLES BATHED IN A SPICY SAUCE OF BEEF STOCK, SOY SAUCE, GINGER, GARLIC AND CHILLI FLAKES.

INGREDIENTS

500 g/1 lb 2 oz fillet steak, cut into thin strips

1½ tbsp sesame seeds

125 ml/4 fl oz beef stock

2 tbsp soy sauce

2 tbsp grated fresh ginger

2 garlic cloves, finely chopped

1 tsp cornflour

½ tsp chilli flakes

3 tbsp sesame oil

1 large head of broccoli, cut into florets

1 yellow pepper, deseeded and thinly sliced

1 fresh red chilli, finely sliced

1 tbsp chilli oil, or to taste

wild rice, to serve

1. Mix the beef strips with 1 tablespoon of the sesame seeds in a small bowl.

2. In a separate bowl, stir together the stock, soy sauce, ginger, garlic, cornflour and chilli flakes.

3. Heat 1 tablespoon of the sesame oil in a large wok. Add the beef strips and stir-fry for 2–3 minutes. Remove and set aside, then wipe out the wok with kitchen paper.

4. Heat the remaining sesame oil in the wok, add the broccoli, yellow pepper, red chilli and chilli oil and stir-fry for 2–3 minutes.

5. Stir in the stock mixture, cover and simmer for 2 minutes.

6. Return the beef to the wok and simmer until the juices thicken, stirring occasionally. Cook for a further 1–2 minutes. Sprinkle with the remaining sesame seeds and serve over wild rice.

SPICY FRIED CHICKEN WITH RED CABBAGE & CHILLI COLESLAW

SERVES: 4	PREP TIME: 20 mins, plus marinating	COOK TIME: 35 mins

INSTEAD OF THE USUAL BREADCRUMBS, THIS CHICKEN HAS A CRUNCHY COATING OF POLENTA, QUINOA FLOUR AND WHOLEMEAL FLOUR, WHICH WORKS BRILLIANTLY WITH THE ZINGY FLAVOURS OF THE COLESLAW.

INGREDIENTS

200 ml/7 fl oz soured cream
½ tsp cayenne pepper
1 garlic clove, crushed
4 chicken thighs and 4 chicken drumsticks (about 850 g/1 lb 14 oz)
2 tsp coarse polenta
2 tbsp quinoa flour
2 tbsp wholemeal plain flour
vegetable oil, for deep-frying
sea salt and pepper (optional)

COLESLAW

200 g/7 oz red cabbage, shredded
400 g/14 oz fennel, shredded
1 red chilli, deseeded and thinly sliced lengthways
100 g/3½ oz Greek-style natural yogurt
juice of ¼ lemon

1. Put the soured cream, cayenne and garlic in a large bowl and season well with salt and pepper, if using. Add the chicken and toss well. Cover the bowl with clingfilm and chill in the refrigerator for 2–3 hours, or overnight if you have time.

2. To make the coleslaw, put all the ingredients in a large bowl and toss well, then season with salt and pepper, if using. Cover and chill in the refrigerator.

3. Mix together the polenta and flours on a plate and season with salt and pepper, if using. Half-fill a heavy-based frying pan with oil and place it over a medium-high heat. Heat the oil to 180°C/350°F, or until a cube of bread browns in 30 seconds. While it heats, sprinkle the flour mixture over the chicken.

4. Cook the chicken in two batches, as too much chicken in the pan will make the oil temperature drop. Using tongs, carefully place half the chicken in the oil. Cook for 6–8 minutes, then turn and cook for a further 6–8 minutes, until the coating is a deep golden brown, the chicken is cooked through to the bone, and the juices run clear with no sign of pink when a skewer is inserted into the thickest part of the meat.

5. Using a slotted spoon, transfer the cooked chicken to kitchen paper to drain, then keep warm in a low oven while you cook the second batch.

6. Serve the chicken on a sharing board with the coleslaw.

THAI GREEN
CHICKEN CURRY
& UDON NOODLES

| SERVES: 4 | PREP TIME: 10 mins | COOK TIME: 15 mins |

THAI 'GREEN' CURRY IS SO CHRISTENED BECAUSE OF THE GREEN CHILLIES FROM WHICH IT IS PREPARED – GREEN CURRY PASTE IS USED IN THIS FRAGRANT, CREAMY CURRY AND THE ONE TO THREE TEASPOON OPTION MEANS THAT YOU CAN CALM DOWN OR ACCENTUATE THE HEAT TO YOUR TASTE.

INGREDIENTS

1 tbsp vegetable oil
1 shallot, diced
1–3 tsp Thai green curry paste
450 ml/15 fl oz canned coconut milk
1 tbsp Thai fish sauce
juice of 1 lime
1 tbsp soft light brown sugar
25 g/1 oz fresh basil leaves
25 g/1 oz fresh coriander leaves
450 g/1 lb fresh udon noodles
350 g/12 oz cooked chicken, shredded
3 spring onions, thinly sliced, to garnish

1. Heat the oil in a non-stick frying pan over a medium heat. Add the shallot and cook for 5 minutes, until soft. Add the curry paste and cook, stirring, for 1 minute.

2. Scoop off the thick cream that will have risen to the top of the coconut milk. Add the cream to the pan with the fish sauce, lime juice and sugar. Cook, stirring frequently, for 1–2 minutes. Stir in the remaining coconut milk and bring the mixture to the boil. Reduce the heat to low and simmer, stirring occasionally, for a further 5 minutes, or until the sauce thickens. Remove from the heat and leave to cool slightly. Add the basil and coriander.

3. Transfer the mixture to a food processor, add the basil and coriander to a food processor and process until smooth and bright green. Return the sauce to the pan and reheat over a medium–low heat.

4. Cook the noodles according to the packet instructions and place them in a large serving bowl.

5. Add the chicken and sauce to the noodles and toss to combine. Serve immediately, garnished with the spring onions.

WHOLE TANDOORI CHICKEN

SERVES: 4	PREP TIME: 35 mins, plus marinating	COOK TIME: 55 mins

THIS DISH ORIGINATES IN THE PUNJAB. THE 'TANDOORI' IN THE NAME COMES FROM THE TANDOOR, A CYLINDRICAL CLAY OVEN, WHERE THIS CHICKEN DISH IS TRADITIONALLY PREPARED AT A VERY HIGH TEMPERATURE.

INGREDIENTS

1 chicken, 1.5 kg/3 lb 5 oz
2 tsp garam masala
300 ml/10 fl oz natural yogurt
1 onion, finely chopped
2 garlic cloves, crushed
2.5-cm/1-inch piece fresh ginger, peeled and grated
juice of 1 lemon
2 tbsp tomato purée
1 tsp chilli powder
1 tsp ground cumin
1 tsp ground turmeric
1 tbsp paprika (not smoked)
1 tsp salt

TO SERVE
basmati rice
naan bread
lime wedges
hot lime pickle

1. Cut two slits into each chicken leg and two into each thigh. They should just reach the bone. Make two shallower cuts into the fleshiest part of each breast. These are to allow the marinade to penetrate into the meat.

2. Mix all of the remaining ingredients together in a food processor and blend to a smooth paste. Place the chicken in a large, non-metallic dish and cover it in the paste, massaging it deep into the skin and flesh. Place the chicken, uncovered, in the refrigerator to marinate for as long as possible – preferably 24 hours.

3. Remove the chicken from the refrigerator an hour before cooking to warm it to room temperature. Preheat the oven to 220°C/425°F/Gas Mark 7. Place the chicken in the oven and cook, uncovered, for 20 minutes, then reduce the heat to 180°C/350°F/Gas Mark 4. Baste the chicken and cook for another 35 minutes. When fully cooked the juices will run clear when a skewer is inserted into the thickest part of the meat. Turn off the oven and open the door, leaving the chicken inside to rest for 20 minutes. Serve with rice, naan bread, lime wedges and lime pickle.

SPICY RICE WITH CHICKEN & POMEGRANATE

| SERVES: 4 | PREP TIME: 25 mins | COOK TIME: 1 hr |

SPICE UP YOUR LUNCH WITH THIS VERY TEMPTING CHICKEN AND RICE DISH, FINISHED WITH FLESHY, PINK POMEGRANATE SEEDS, WHICH PACK A POWERFUL NUTRIENT PUNCH, PLUS VIVID, GREEN, ANTIOXIDANT-RICH FRESH HERBS.

INGREDIENTS

4 large chicken thighs
2 tsp Chinese five spice
2 tbsp olive oil
2 red onions, finely sliced
2 garlic cloves, finely sliced
5 cardamom pods, crushed
2 star anise
250 g/9 oz brown rice
750 ml/1¼ pints vegetable stock
25 g/1 oz fresh mint, roughly chopped
25 g/1 oz fresh flat-leaf parsley, roughly chopped
seeds of 1 small pomegranate
4 tbsp toasted almonds
finely grated zest and juice of 1 lemon
salt and pepper (optional)

1. Preheat the oven to 200°C/400°F/Gas Mark 6. Place the chicken thighs on a baking tray and sprinkle over the Chinese five spice. Drizzle over 1 tablespoon of olive oil and roast in the preheated oven for 20 minutes, or until the juices run clear when the thickest part of the meat is pierced and no traces of pink remain in the centre. Remove from the oven and set aside to cool.

2. Meanwhile, heat the remaining tablespoon of olive oil in a large saucepan over a medium–low heat. Add the onion and gently fry for 10–12 minutes, or until soft and starting to caramelize. Stir in the garlic, cardamom pods and star anise and cook for a further minute. Add the rice and stir well.

3. Pour in the stock and bring the pan to the boil. Cover and simmer gently for 25–30 minutes, or until all the stock has been absorbed and the rice is tender.

4. Once the chicken is cool enough to handle, remove the meat from the bones and finely slice. Add to the rice mixture, with any remaining juices, and season with salt and pepper, if using.

5. Stir in half of the mint and parsley. Top with the remaining herbs, pomegranate seeds, toasted almonds, lemon juice and zest and serve immediately.

SPICES FROM
DRIED FRUITS & SEEDS

A spice is 'a seed, fruit, root, bark, berry, bud or other vegetable substance used for flavouring, colouring or preserving'. Chilli is classed as a spice, but there are many others from which to choose.

The spice trade was a significant driving force within the world economy from the end of the Middle Ages, the most common and popular spices in the medieval period including black pepper (the most expensive), cinnamon, cumin, nutmeg, ginger and cloves. Spices can be created from different plant forms – from dried fruits or seeds, such as mustard, nutmeg, fennel and black pepper; arils such as mace; barks such as cassia and cinnamon; dried flower buds such as cloves; stigmas such as saffron; and roots such as turmeric and ginger. Here we look at spices that are sourced from dried fruits or seeds.

Allspice also called pimento, is an aromatic spice created from the dried unripe berry of the West Indian allspice tree. It was called 'allspice' as it was felt to capture the flavours of cinnamon, nutmeg and cloves. It is used widely in Caribbean cuisine, especially in jerk seasoning and mole sauces.

Black pepper is the dried fruit of a flowering vine in the *Piperaceae* family and peppercorns are a familiar feature in every kitchen. First grown in southern India, it is commonly used to enhance the appetite and give dishes a warming quality.

Cayenne pepper is from the chilli family and the dried fruit is commonly used in its powdered form after the peppers are dried and ground and sifted to create the powder that gives heat to spicy dishes.

Cumin seeds are small seeds, a similar size to rice grains, taken from the plant *Cuminum cyminum*. They have a warm and slightly bitter quality and are used widely in South Asian, North African and Latin American cuisines. Cumin is available in whole and ground form.

Fennel is a dried, oval-shaped seed that comes from the herb *Foeniculum vulgare*, which is distinctive for its aniseed flavour (see opposite, above right). Fennel seeds can be brown or green – green seeds are the best choice for cooking.

Mustard seeds are the fruit pods of the mustard plant and are available as black, brown, yellow or white seeds. They have a nutty taste and are used extensively in Indian cooking.

Nutmeg is the seed of the nutmeg tree, *Myristica fragrans* (see opposite, below), which is indigenous to the Spice Islands in Indonesia. It has a comforting spicy warmth and is usually used in powdered form. It is equally useful in sweet and savoury dishes.

Paprika originated in central Mexico and is made from the air-dried fruits of the chilli pepper, which are then formed into a powder. Bright red, it is often used to add colour to dishes. It is available in different strengths, but is milder than cayenne pepper, and has a sweet quality.

Star anise is the dried fruit of an evergreen tree called *Illicium velum* native to southwest China (see opposite, above left). It has a distinctive eight-pointed star shape and contains anethole, an oil with an aniseed flavour. It is widely used in Chinese and Indian cuisine.

MEXICAN
TURKEY BURGERS

| SERVES: 4 | PREP TIME: 25 mins, plus chilling | COOK TIME: 20 mins |

THESE DELICIOUS ROAST BURGERS ARE IDEAL FOR A BARBECUE, OR CAN EASILY BE PREPARED IN THE KITCHEN TO GIVE A BARBECUE FLAVOUR TO AN INDOOR MEAL.

INGREDIENTS

450 g/1 lb fresh turkey mince

200 g/7 oz canned refried beans

2–4 garlic cloves, crushed

1–2 fresh jalapeño chillies, deseeded and finely chopped

2 tbsp tomato purée

1 tbsp chopped fresh coriander

1 tbsp sunflower oil

salt and pepper

shredded baby spinach leaves

TO SERVE

4 cheese-topped burger buns, split

salsa

guacamole

tortilla chips

1. Place the turkey mince in a bowl and break up any large lumps. Beat the refried beans until smooth, then add them to the turkey in the bowl.

2. Add the garlic, chillies, tomato purée and coriander with salt and pepper to taste and mix together. Shape into four equal-sized patties, then cover and leave to chill in the refrigerator for 1 hour.

3. Preheat the barbecue, if using. Otherwise, add the oil to a large pan on medium–high heat, until hot. Add the burgers and cook for 5–6 minutes on each side, or until browned and cooked through. If barbecuing, brush the patties with the oil and cook over medium-hot coals for 5–6 minutes on each side, or until cooked through.

4. Place the spinach on the bottom halves of the burger buns and top with the burgers. Spoon over a little salsa and guacamole and top with the lids. Serve immediately with tortilla chips on the side.

SPICED TURKEY STEW WITH WHOLEGRAIN COUSCOUS

SERVES: 4	PREP TIME: 20 mins	COOK TIME: 25 mins

CAPTURE THE FLAVOURS OF MIDDLE EASTERN COOKING WITH THIS EASY, LIGHTLY SPICED STOVE-TOP TURKEY STEW.

INGREDIENTS

1 tbsp virgin olive oil

500 g/1 lb 2 oz skinless and boneless turkey breast, cut into 2-cm/¾-inch pieces

1 onion, roughly chopped

2 garlic cloves, finely chopped

1 red pepper, deseeded and roughly chopped

1 orange pepper, deseeded and roughly chopped

500 g/1 lb 2 oz tomatoes, roughly chopped

1 tsp cumin seeds, roughly crushed

1 tsp paprika

zest and juice of 1 unwaxed lemon

sea salt and pepper (optional)

TO SERVE

200 g/7 oz wholegrain giant couscous

2 tbsp roughly chopped fresh flat-leaf parsley

2 tbsp roughly chopped fresh coriander

1. Heat the oil in a large frying pan over a medium heat. Add the turkey, a few pieces at a time, then add the onion. Fry, stirring, for 5 minutes, or until the turkey is golden.

2. Add the garlic, red and orange peppers and tomatoes, then stir in the cumin seeds and paprika. Add the lemon juice and season with salt and pepper, if using. Stir well, then cover and cook, stirring from time to time, for 20 minutes, or until the tomatoes have formed a thick sauce and the turkey is cooked through and the juices run clear with no sign of pink when a piece is cut in half.

3. Meanwhile, half-fill a saucepan with water and bring to the boil. Add the couscous and cook according to the packet instructions, or until just tender. Tip into a sieve and drain well.

4. Spoon the couscous onto plates and top with the turkey stew. Mix the parsley and coriander with the lemon zest, then sprinkle over the stew and serve.

PORK WITH CHILLIES, VINEGAR & GARLIC

SERVES: 4	PREP TIME: 10 mins, plus chilling	COOK TIME: 1¼–1½ hrs

WHEN THE PORTUGUESE TRAVELLED TO INDIA, THEY TOOK PORK PRESERVED IN VINEGAR, GARLIC AND PEPPER, WHICH WAS SPICED UP TO SUIT INDIAN TASTES AND THIS VINDALOO DISH WAS BORN.

INGREDIENTS

2–6 dried red chillies, torn

5 cloves

2.5-cm/1-inch piece cinnamon stick, broken up

4 green cardamom pods

½ tsp black peppercorns

½ mace blade

¼ nutmeg, grated

1 tsp cumin seeds

1½ tsp coriander seeds

½ tsp fenugreek seeds

2 tsp garlic paste

1 tbsp ginger paste

3 tbsp cider vinegar or white wine vinegar

1 tbsp tamarind juice or juice of ½ lime

700 g/1 lb 9 oz boneless pork leg, cut into 2.5-cm/1-inch cubes

4 tbsp vegetable or groundnut oil, plus 2 tsp

2 large onions, finely chopped

300 ml/10 fl oz warm water

1 tsp salt, or to taste

1 tsp soft dark brown sugar

2 large garlic cloves, finely sliced

8–10 fresh curry leaves

1. Grind the first ten ingredients (all the spices) to a fine powder in a spice grinder. Transfer the ground spices to a bowl and add the garlic and ginger pastes, vinegar and tamarind juice. Mix together to form a paste.

2. Put the pork in a large, non-metallic bowl and rub about one quarter of the spice paste into the meat. Cover and leave to marinate in the refrigerator for 30–40 minutes.

3. Heat the 4 tablespoons of oil in a heavy-based saucepan over a medium heat, add the onions and cook, stirring frequently, for 8–10 minutes, until lightly browned. Add the remaining spice paste and cook, stirring constantly, for 5–6 minutes. Add 2 tablespoons of the water and cook until it evaporates. Repeat with another 2 tablespoons of water.

4. Add the marinated pork and cook over a medium-high heat for 5–6 minutes. Add the salt, sugar and the remaining water. Bring to the boil, then reduce the heat to low, cover and simmer for 50–55 minutes.

5. Meanwhile, heat the 2 teaspoons of oil in a small saucepan over a low heat. Add the sliced garlic and cook, stirring, until it begins to brown. Add the curry leaves and leave to sizzle for 15–20 seconds. Stir the garlic mixture into the pan. Serve immediately.

RIB OF BEEF WITH A FIERY HORSERADISH CRUST

| SERVES: 4–6 | PREP TIME: 10 mins | COOK TIME: 60 mins, plus resting |

A COATING OF SPICY CREAMED HORSERADISH AND MUSTARD MAKES THIS SUCCULENT RIB INTO SOMETHING EXTRA SPECIAL. CARVE IT FOR A ROAST DINNER AND ANY LEFTOVERS WILL BE DELICIOUS SERVED COLD.

INGREDIENTS

2 kg/4 lb 8 oz rib of beef on the bone
1 tsp salt
1 tsp pepper
4 tbsp olive oil

HORSERADISH CRUST

2 tbsp extra virgin olive oil
4 tbsp creamed horseradish
2 tbsp English mustard
zest and juice of 1 lemon
½ tsp salt
½ tsp pepper

1. Preheat the oven to 180°C/350°F/Gas Mark 4.

2. Place the beef rib on a large chopping board and season with the salt and pepper.

3. Place all of the horseradish crust ingredients into a small bowl and mix until combined to a rough paste.

4. Heat the olive oil in a large frying pan over a medium-high heat and seal the rib on all sides. Transfer to a wire rack positioned over a roasting tray and brush all over with the horseradish paste. Place the tray in the preheated oven and cook for 50 minutes.

5. Remove the rib from the oven and set aside to rest for 30 minutes before serving. Serve with the juices from the roasting tray poured over.

COLOSSAL LAMB KEBAB WITH HOT CHILLI SAUCE

| SERVES: 1 | PREP TIME: 10 mins | COOK TIME: 10 mins |

THESE SPICY HOT LAMB KEBABS ARE SERIOUSLY SIMPLE AND SERIOUSLY FILLING. PERFECT FOR THE BARBECUE OR FOR A SOLO EVENING MEAL, THE KEBAB AND CHILLI SAUCE CAN ALSO BE SERVED WITH HOT PITTA BREAD.

INGREDIENTS

500 g/1 lb 2 oz leg of lamb, diced

2 tbsp olive oil

1 tsp dried thyme

1 tsp paprika

1 tsp ground cumin

1 large flatbread

1 small red onion, sliced

1 tomato, chopped

small bunch of fresh coriander, chopped

½ lemon

salt and pepper

sriracha or other hot chilli sauce and natural yogurt, to serve

1. In a medium-sized bowl mix the lamb with the olive oil, thyme and spices and season to taste with salt and pepper.

2. Preheat a large griddle pan or barbecue.

3. Thread the lamb onto two large skewers, and cook in the preheated pan for 4-5 minutes on each side, or until cooked to your liking.

4. Heat a large, dry frying pan and cook the flatbread for a few seconds on both sides until soft.

5. Remove the lamb from the skewers, place on the flatbread and top with the onion, tomato and coriander. Squeeze over the lemon and serve immediately with the sriracha and natural yogurt.

LAMB WITH
BLACK BEAN SAUCE

| SERVES: 4 | PREP TIME: 25 mins | COOK TIME: 12–14 mins |

FIVE-SPICE POWDER AND BLACK BEAN SAUCE CREATE SOME MAGIC WITH LAMB AND PEPPERS TO GIVE THIS DISH PLENTY OF WARMTH AND PIZAZZ.

INGREDIENTS

450 g/1 lb lamb neck fillet or boneless leg of lamb chops

1 egg white, lightly beaten

4 tbsp cornflour

1 tsp Chinese five-spice powder

3 tbsp sunflower oil

1 red onion, sliced

1 red pepper, deseeded and sliced

1 green pepper, deseeded and sliced

1 yellow or orange pepper, deseeded and sliced

5 tbsp black bean sauce

freshly cooked noodles, to serve

1. Using a sharp knife, slice the lamb into very thin strips.

2. Mix together the egg white, cornflour and Chinese five-spice powder. Toss the lamb strips in the mixture until evenly coated.

3. Heat the oil in a preheated wok or large frying pan and stir-fry the lamb over a high heat for 5 minutes, or until it crisps around the edges.

4. Add the onion and pepper slices to the wok and stir-fry for 5–6 minutes, or until the vegetables just begin to soften.

5. Stir the black bean sauce into the lamb mixture in the wok and heat through.

6. Transfer the lamb and sauce to warm serving plates and serve hot with freshly cooked noodles.

TIP

BLACK BEAN SAUCE IS MADE WITH SALTY FERMENTED BEANS. CHECK THE FINISHED DISH FOR FLAVOUR BEFORE ADDING ANY EXTRA SALT.

FISH & SEAFOOD MAINS

When you're in the mood for a taste of the sea, these zingy fishy dishes will deliver a spicy punch of flavours to satisfy your cravings. Including prawns, crayfish, scallops and sardines, the succulent recipes feature Maharashtrian Salmon Curry, Prawn & Chilli-Lime Spaghetti, Whole Spice-Crusted Red Snapper, and Crayfish Cakes with Avocado & Chilli Mash.

MAHARASHTRIAN
SALMON CURRY

| SERVES: 4 | PREP TIME: 5–10 mins | COOK TIME: 15–20 mins |

THIS SIMPLE FISH CURRY IS PACKED WITH FLAVOUR. YOU CAN USE ANY FIRM FISH FILLET OR FISH STEAKS INSTEAD OF THE SALMON, IF DESIRED. SERVE WITH FRESHLY COOKED BASMATI RICE TO SOAK UP THE DELICIOUS COOKING LIQUID.

INGREDIENTS

6 tbsp vegetable or groundnut oil

8 salmon steaks, each weighing about 150 g/5½ oz

2 tsp cornflour

1 tsp hot chilli powder

1 tsp paprika

½ tsp ground turmeric

2 tsp ground cumin

1 tsp ground coriander

2 tsp salt

1 tsp tamarind paste

400 ml/14 fl oz coconut milk

400 ml/14 fl oz cold water

1. Heat the oil in a non-stick saucepan and add the fish. Fry for 1–2 minutes on each side.

2. Mix together the cornflour, spices, salt, tamarind paste and coconut milk. Pour this mixture into the saucepan with the water.

3. Bring to the boil, then reduce the heat, cover and cook gently for 10–12 minutes, or until the fish is cooked through and the sauce has thickened slightly (it should still be quite runny). Serve immediately.

SPICED BAKED COD
WITH HARISSA & PINE NUT CRUST
& ROAST CHERRY TOMATOES

SERVES: 2	PREP TIME: 10 mins	COOK TIME: 15 mins

THIS DISH IS INCREDIBLY QUICK TO PREPARE, AND MAKES A DELICIOUS, EASY MIDWEEK MEAL. THE SPICY, CRUNCHY TOPPING CONTRASTS BEAUTIFULLY WITH THE SOFT FISH FLAKES.

INGREDIENTS

30 g/1 oz pine nuts

15 g/½ oz breadcrumbs

grated zest of 1 unwaxed lemon

2 tbsp roughly chopped
fresh coriander

pinch of sea salt

1 tsp olive oil

200 g/7 oz cherry tomatoes
on the vine

2 cod fillets, about 200 g/7 oz each

2 tsp rose harissa

1. Preheat the oven to 200°C/400°F/Gas Mark 6. Crush the pine nuts in a pestle and mortar. Tip them into a bowl, add the breadcrumbs, lemon zest, coriander, salt and oil and mix well.

2. Put the cherry tomatoes on a large baking tray and add the cod fillets skin-side down, arranging everything in a single layer. Spread a teaspoon of rose harissa over each cod fillet, then top with the breadcrumb mixture, pressing down gently.

3. Bake on a high shelf in the oven for 15 minutes, or until the topping is crisp and golden and the fish flakes easily when pressed with a knife. Serve the cod hot with the tomatoes.

TIP

SUBSTITUTE POLLACK, COLEY OR ANY OTHER FIRM WHITE FISH FOR THE COD – WHATEVER IS FRESHEST AND BEST VALUE ON THE DAY.

MOROCCAN FISH TAGINE

SERVES: 4	PREP TIME: 20 mins	COOK TIME: 55 mins–1¼ hours

PREPARED WITH RED MULLET, THIS TAGINE IS FULL OF RICH FLAVOURS AND SPICY WARMTH PRODUCED BY THE RICH COMBINATION OF SPICES.

INGREDIENTS

2 tbsp olive oil

1 large onion, finely chopped

pinch of saffron threads

½ tsp ground cinnamon

1 tsp ground coriander

½ tsp ground cumin

½ tsp ground turmeric

200 g/7 oz canned chopped tomatoes

300 ml/10 fl oz fish stock

4 small red mullet, cleaned, boned and heads and tails removed

55 g/2 oz stoned green olives

1 tbsp chopped preserved lemon

3 tbsp chopped fresh coriander

salt and pepper (optional)

couscous, to serve

1. Heat the oil in a flameproof casserole. Add the onion and cook over a very low heat, stirring occasionally, for 10 minutes, until soft, but not coloured. Add the saffron, cinnamon, ground coriander, cumin and turmeric and cook the mixture for a further 30 seconds, stirring constantly.

2. Add the tomatoes and fish stock and stir well. Bring to the boil, reduce the heat, cover and simmer for 15 minutes. Uncover and simmer for 20–35 minutes, or until thickened.

3. Cut each red mullet in half, then add the fish pieces to the casserole, pushing them down into the liquid. Simmer the stew for a further 5–6 minutes, or until the fish is just cooked.

4. Carefully stir in the olives, preserved lemon and chopped coriander. Season to taste with salt and pepper, if using, and serve with couscous.

PRAWN & CHILLI-LIME SPAGHETTI

SERVES: 4	PREP TIME: 20–30 mins	COOK TIME: 30 mins

THIS DISH, COMBINING PLUMP, JUICY PRAWNS, COURGETTES AND SPAGHETTI, WITH THE ADDED BITE OF JALAPEÑO CHILLIES, PROVIDES AN EASY MEAL.

INGREDIENTS

1–2 tsp salt
450 g/1 lb dried spaghetti
4 garlic cloves
2–4 red or green jalapeño chillies
4 small courgettes
3 spring onions
2 tbsp olive oil
450 g/1 lb peeled and deveined raw prawns
finely grated zest and juice of 1 lime
2 tbsp butter
salt (optional)

1. Add the salt to a large saucepan of water and bring to the boil, add the spaghetti, bring back to the boil and cook for 8–10 minutes, or until tender but still firm to the bite. Meanwhile, peel and crush the garlic, deseed and dice the chillies, dice the courgettes and thinly slice the spring onions.

2. Drain the pasta in a colander and set aside until needed. Return the pan to the heat, add the oil and heat over a medium-high heat. Add the garlic and cook, stirring, for 1–2 minutes, until it begins to soften. Add the chillies, courgettes and salt, if using, and cook, stirring occasionally, until the courgettes are beginning to brown.

3. Add the prawns and lime juice and zest to the pan. Add the spring onions and cook, stirring occasionally, until the prawns are pink and cooked through. Add the butter and the reserved spaghetti and cook, stirring, for 1–2 minutes, until most of the liquid has evaporated. Serve immediately.

DEEP-FRIED FISH WITH CHILLI BEAN SAUCE

SERVES: 4–6	PREP TIME: 25 mins	COOK TIME: 20–25 mins

DEEP-FRIED FRESHWATER FISH WITH A TEMPTING SAUCE THAT COMBINES THE FLAVOURS OF CHILLI, GARLIC, GINGER AND CHILLI BEAN OFFERS UP A DIVINE TREAT WITH A BIT OF A KICK.

INGREDIENTS

4 whole freshwater fish, such as trout or carp, weighing around 400 g/14 oz, gutted

1 heaped tbsp plain flour

pinch of salt

100 ml/3½ fl oz water

vegetable or groundnut oil, for deep-frying

SAUCE

100 ml/3½ fl oz vegetable or groundnut oil

1 tsp dried chilli flakes

1 garlic clove, finely chopped

1 tsp finely chopped fresh ginger

1 tbsp chilli bean sauce

½ tsp white pepper

2 tsp sugar

1 tbsp white rice vinegar

1 tsp finely chopped spring onion

1. To prepare the fish, clean and dry thoroughly. Mix together the flour, salt and water to create a light batter. Coat the fish.

2. Heat enough oil for deep-frying in a wok, deep-fat fryer or large heavy-based saucepan to 180–190°C/350–375°F, or until a cube of bread browns in 30 seconds. Deep-fry the fish until the skin is crisp and golden brown. Drain, set aside and keep warm.

3. To make the sauce, first heat all but 1 tablespoon of the oil in a small pan and, when smoking, pour over the chilli flakes. Set aside.

4. In a preheated wok or deep pan, heat the remaining oil and stir-fry the garlic and ginger until fragrant. Stir in the chilli bean sauce, then add the oil-chilli flake mixture. Season with the pepper, sugar and vinegar. Turn off the heat and stir in the spring onion. Tip over the fish and serve immediately.

FISH IN TOMATO & CHILLI
SAUCE WITH FRIED ONION

| SERVES: 4 | PREP TIME: 10 mins, plus marinating | COOK TIME: 35–40 mins |

FIRM-FLESHED FISH IS SHALLOW-FRIED UNTIL BROWNED AND THEN SIMMERED IN AN ALLURINGLY SPICED CHILLI AND TOMATO SAUCE. THIS DISH IS BEST SERVED WITH FRESHLY COOKED BASMATI RICE AND POPPADOMS.

INGREDIENTS

700 g/1 lb 9 oz white fish fillets, such as sole, cod or haddock, cut into 5-cm/2-inch pieces

2 tbsp lemon juice

1 tsp salt, or to taste

1 tsp ground turmeric

4 tbsp vegetable or groundnut oil, plus extra for shallow-frying

2 tsp sugar

1 large onion, finely chopped

2 tsp ginger paste

2 tsp garlic paste

½ tsp ground fennel seeds

1 tsp ground coriander

½–1 tsp chilli powder

175 g/6 oz canned chopped tomatoes

300 ml/10 fl oz warm water

2–3 tbsp chopped fresh coriander

1. Place the fish on a large plate and gently rub in the lemon juice, ½ teaspoon of the salt and ½ teaspoon of the turmeric. Set aside for 15–20 minutes.

2. Pour enough oil into a frying pan to fill to a depth of about 1 cm/½ inch and place over a medium–high heat. When the oil is hot, fry the pieces of fish, in a single layer, until well browned on both sides and a light crust is formed. Drain on kitchen paper.

3. Heat the 4 tablespoons of oil in a saucepan or frying pan over a medium heat and add the sugar. Allow it to brown, watching it carefully because once it browns it will blacken quickly. As soon as the sugar is brown, add the onion and cook for 5 minutes, until soft. Add the ginger and garlic pastes and cook for a further 3–4 minutes, or until the mixture begins to brown.

4. Add the ground fennel seeds, ground coriander, chilli powder and the remaining turmeric. Cook for about a minute, then add half the tomatoes. Stir and cook until the tomato juice has evaporated, then add the remaining tomatoes. Continue to cook, stirring, until the oil separates from the spice paste.

5. Pour in the water and add the remaining salt. Bring to the boil and reduce the heat to medium. Add the fish, stir gently and reduce the heat to low. Cook, uncovered, for 5–6 minutes, then stir in half the chopped coriander and remove from the heat. Garnish with the remaining coriander and serve immediately.

GROW YOUR OWN CHILLIES

We know you love the taste of chillies…but did you realize they're easy to grow yourself? It is not necessary to live in a hot country or near the Equator – with a little bit of care, anyone can nurture a crop!

The best news for aspiring chilli growers is that you don't need a garden – chillies are best grown in pots so any little amount of outdoor space should suffice, even a windowsill or a hanging pot.

1. Plant in January to harvest in July – but start them off indoors. In the UK it is too cold outside for your little chilli plants until at least mid-May.

2. Fill a seed tray with compost, lightly water and place a seed in each cell or compartment of the tray. Put a bit more compost on top. Water again, cover with clingfilm and place somewhere warm such as an airing cupboard. Check them every day and keep them moist.

3. After about a month you should see some sprouts coming through (see opposite, above left). Remove the clingfilm and move them to a warm windowsill. Keep moist.

4. When your seedlings sprout a second set of leaves, carefully transplant them to small pots – and encourage growth with a weekly tomato feed.

5. At about 13 cm/5 inches tall, transplant the plants to bigger pots. Support any drooping plants by tying them to a cane, important because their roots are shallow. Locate peppers in full sun in a rich, organic-based soil that is moisture retentive and drains well.

6. Try not to let your plants grow much above a foot tall – if you pinch the tops above the leaves then you will encourage bushiness and more flowers.

7. As the plants develop, flowers will start to appear on your plants.

8. Start feeding with a liquid fertilizer once the flowers appear, or just before they start to form, and carry on until the fruit has been harvested. Feed them every two weeks.

9. After flowering, the flowers will go brown and drop off. This is quite normal and indicates that a chilli is pushing its way through the flower. Keep the plant fed and watered as the chillies ripen.

10. Harvest your chilli peppers by removing them from plants with a sharp knife or secateurs to prevent any damage to the plant. Snip off (and eat) the first crop while they're stilll green – this will encourage regrowth.

TOP TIPS

Water chilli plants regularly, especially in hot weather. Chilli plants thrive in the light, so give them plenty to ensure a fast, strong growth.

Pick fruit regularly to make sure that the plant can direct its resources towards producing more fruit.

The best colour and flavour will come from chillies that are left to ripen to a good colour, but be aware that leaving fruit on the plant will suppress new fruit from coming through.

Fresh hot peppers will keep in the refrigerator for 1 week or in a cool, dry position for up to 2 weeks.

MONKFISH & BABY BROCCOLI
COCONUT CURRY

| SERVES: 4 | PREP TIME: 15 mins | COOK TIME: 20 mins |

FISH, COCONUT, AND SPICES WERE SIMPLY MADE FOR EACH OTHER, AS YOU'LL KNOW IF YOU TRY THIS QUICK-AND-SIMPLE CURRY FOR DINNER.

INGREDIENTS

1 large onion, chopped
2 tsp fish sauce
juice of ½ lime
1 red chilli, de-stalked
1 green chilli, de-stalked
2 tsp crushed coriander seeds
2 tsp crushed cumin seeds
2.5-cm/1-inch piece fresh ginger, chopped
3 garlic cloves, roughly chopped
½ lemon grass stalk
1½ tbsp groundnut oil
5 curry leaves
300 ml/10 fl oz coconut milk
350 g/12 oz purple sprouting broccoli, each spear cut into 2 pieces
500 g/1 lb 2 oz monkfish fillet, cubed
1 red chilli, sliced

1. Add the onion, fish sauce, lime juice, de-stalked chillies, seeds, ginger, garlic, lemon grass and half of the oil to the bowl of a blender or food processor and process until you have a paste. Tip the mixture into a frying pan and cook over a medium heat for 2 minutes. Stir in the curry leaves and coconut milk and simmer for 10 more minutes.

2. Meanwhile, add the remaining oil to another frying pan and place over a high heat. Stir-fry the broccoli for 2 minutes, or until just tender. Set aside.

3. Add the monkfish cubes to the curry pan and bring back to a simmer. Cook for 2 minutes, then add the broccoli spears to the pan and continue cooking for a further minute. Serve the curry with the sliced chilli sprinkled over the top.

WHOLE SPICE-CRUSTED RED SNAPPER

| SERVES: 2 | PREP TIME: 10 mins | COOK TIME: 20 mins |

THE SPICES HERE HAVE JUST THE RIGHT AMOUNT OF HEAT AND FLAVOUR TO COMPLEMENT THE FISH AND GIVE IT A CRISP CRUST THAT CONTRASTS WITH ITS SOFT FLESH. THE RECIPE IS EASILY SCALED UP IF YOU'RE COOKING FOR MORE THAN TWO PEOPLE. SERVE WITH STEAMED VEGETABLES OR SAMPHIRE.

INGREDIENTS

2 whole red snapper, scaled and gutted

1 lemon, thinly sliced

3½ tsp dukkah spice

60 g/2¼ oz ground almonds

4 tbsp olive oil

4 tbsp finely chopped fresh coriander

2 tsp sea salt flakes

grated zest of 1 unwaxed lemon

1. Preheat the oven to 200°C/400°F/Gas Mark 6. Line a large roasting tin with baking paper and lay the fish on top.

2. Mix the lemon zest, dukkah spice, ground almonds, oil, coriander and salt together in a bowl.

3. Spoon 2 tablespoons of the mixture over one side of each fish, pressing it down gently to make a crust. Turn each fish over and spoon 2 tablespoons of the mixture on the other side. Put any remaining mixture in the cavities. Divide the lemon slices between the cavities.

4. Roast for 20 minutes, or until the fish flakes easily when tested with a knife. Leave to rest for 2 minutes before serving hot.

TIP

WHEN BUYING WHOLE FISH, LOOK FOR BRIGHT AND CLEAR EYES, SHINY SKIN, AND BRIGHT-RED GILLS, AND MAKE SURE IT SMELLS FRESH.

CRAYFISH CAKES
WITH AVOCADO & CHILLI MASH

SERVES: 4	PREP TIME: 15 mins, plus chilling	COOK TIME: 5–10 mins

TASTY CRAYFISH TAILS ARE A DELIGHTFULLY LOW-FAT TREAT AND, ALTHOUGH THEY DO CONTAIN CHOLESTEROL, THEY CAN BE ENJOYED AS PART OF A BALANCED, HEART-FRIENDLY DIET.

INGREDIENTS

30 g/1 oz wholemeal breadcrumbs

½ tsp pepper

2 tbsp finely chopped fresh flat-leaf parsley

200 g/7 oz peeled and cooked crayfish tails, roughly chopped

50 g/1¾ oz ready-roasted red pepper from a jar, drained and chopped

1 tsp medium-hot peri peri sauce

1 tbsp extra-light mayonnaise

1 small egg white, beaten

10 g/¼ oz flour, for dusting

6 sprays cooking oil spray

AVOCADO & CHILLI MASH

1 ripe avocado, peeled, stoned and sliced

1 small fresh red chilli, deseeded and finely chopped

1 spring onion, finely chopped

½ tsp smoked paprika

juice of ¼ lime

1. Put the breadcrumbs, pepper and parsley into a bowl and stir well to combine.

2. In a separate bowl, combine the crayfish tails, red pepper, peri peri sauce and mayonnaise. Stir the breadcrumb mixture into the crayfish mixture.

3. Add the beaten egg white and mix to a moderately firm mixture – the cakes will firm up more once they are cooked. Divide into four rough rounds and sprinkle with flour. If you have time, chill for up to 1 hour.

4. To make the mash, place the avocado slices in a bowl and roughly mash with a fork. Stir in the chilli, spring onion, paprika and lime juice.

5. Spray a nonstick frying pan with the cooking oil spray and place over a medium-high heat. Add the crayfish cakes and cook for 2–3 minutes, or until the underside is crisp and golden. Turn and cook for a further 2–3 minutes, or until cooked through. Serve the cakes immediately with the avocado mash on the side.

FISH WITH CHILLI, WHITE WINE & TAPENADE

SERVES: 4	PREP TIME: 5 mins	COOK TIME: 15 mins

THIS FISH, CHILLI AND TAPENADE DISH IS A BREEZE TO PREPARE AND YET IT ALSO DELIVERS SOME SOPHISTICATED FLAVOURS.

INGREDIENTS

1 tbsp olive oil

4 white fish fillets

4 tbsp tapenade

1 small red finger chilli, deseeded and chopped

4 tbsp freshly grated Parmesan cheese

4 tbsp dry white wine

salt and pepper (optional)

720 g/1 lb 9½ oz cooked rice, to serve

1. Preheat the oven to 220°C/425°F/Gas Mark 7. Brush a wide, ovenproof dish with the oil.

2. Season the fish with salt and pepper, if using, and place in the prepared dish in a single layer.

3. Mix the tapenade and chilli together and spread over the fish, then sprinkle with the cheese.

4. Pour the wine around the fish and bake in the preheated oven for about 15 minutes, or until the flesh flakes easily. Serve with the rice.

SEARED SCALLOPS
WITH FRESH MINT
& RED CHILLI DRESSING

| SERVES: 4–6 | PREP TIME: 35 mins | COOK TIME: 25–28 mins |

ENJOY THESE SEARED SCALLOPS ON A BED OF PEPPERY SALAD, WITH HERBY PUY LENTILS, PAN-FRIED PANCETTA AND A DRIZZLE OF MINT-CHILLI DRESSING.

INGREDIENTS

100 g/3½ oz Puy lentils

2 garlic cloves

1 celery stick

2 bay leaves

20 fresh parsley leaves, with stalks

olive oil, for drizzling and frying

zest and juice of 1 lemon

2 tbsp aged red wine vinegar

20 fresh basil leaves, roughly chopped

20 fresh mint leaves, roughly chopped

handful of rocket leaves, roughly chopped

20 scallops

8 slices pancetta

salt and pepper (optional)

peppery salad leaves, to serve

MINT & RED CHILLI DRESSING

2 red chillies, deseeded and chopped

small bunch of fresh mint, finely chopped

100 ml/3½ fl oz extra virgin olive oil

juice of 1 lemon

salt and pepper (optional)

1. Cover the lentils with water in a large pan and add the garlic, celery stick, bay leaves and a few parsley stalks. Bring to the boil, then reduce to a simmer.

2. Cook the lentils for 12–15 minutes, until they are al dente and nutty. Remove from the heat and drain off most of the water. Remove the garlic, bay leaves, celery stick and parsley stalks. Season the lentils with olive oil, lemon zest and juice, some of the vinegar, and salt and pepper, if using.

3. When the lentils have cooled slightly, add the herbs and rocket and stir until combined. Set the lentils aside.

4. For the dressing, mix together the chillies and mint in a bowl with the olive oil and the lemon juice, and season with salt and pepper, if using.

5. Clean the scallops by removing the small opaque muscle from the sides, and dry them on kitchen paper. Add a tablespoon of oil to a frying pan over a high heat, add the pancetta and fry the slices for 2 minutes on each side, until crispy. Drain on kitchen paper.

6. Keep the frying pan over a high heat. Pat the scallops until dry. Add a splash more olive oil to the frying pan. Add the scallops and cook for 45 seconds. To turn the scallops, quickly use two tablespoons, one in each hand. Flick the scallops over from one spoon to the other. Cook on the second side for about 40 seconds; when the scallops are caramelized on both sides remove and place on clean kitchen paper.

7. Add a splash of vinegar to deglaze the frying pan, then add the liquid to the dressing. To serve, scatter the herb lentils over the salad leaves, arrange the scallops and the pancetta on top. Spoon over some of the mint and chilli dressing and serve immediately.

BAKED FISH
WRAPPED IN BANANA LEAVES

SERVES: 4	PREP TIME: 15–20 mins	COOK TIME: 15–20 mins

THIS DELICIOUS INDIAN BAKED FISH DISH LOOKS PRETTY SERVED WRAPPED UP IN BANANA LEAVES. YOUR GUESTS WILL ENJOY THE MOUTH-WATERING AROMAS THAT ARE RELEASED AS THEY UNWRAP THEIR INDIVIDUAL PACKAGES AT THE TABLE.

INGREDIENTS

4 thick cod fillets, about 200 g/
7 oz each, skinned

2 tsp ground turmeric

1 large fresh banana leaf

SPICE PASTE

2 tsp ground cumin

2 tsp ground coriander

1½ tsp palm sugar

200 ml/7 fl oz coconut cream

4 fresh red chillies, deseeded and chopped

100 g/3½ oz chopped fresh coriander

4 tbsp chopped fresh mint

5 garlic cloves, chopped

1 tsp finely grated fresh ginger

4 tbsp vegetable or groundnut oil

juice of 2 limes

2 tsp salt

1. Preheat the oven to 200°C/400°F/Gas Mark 6.

2. Place the fish fillets in a single layer on a plate and sprinkle over the turmeric. Rub into the fish and set aside.

3. Place the ingredients for the spice paste in a food processor and blend until fairly smooth.

4. Cut the banana leaf into four 24-cm/9½-inch squares. Soften the banana leaf squares by dipping them into a pan of very hot water for a few seconds. Once the banana leaf squares have become pliant, wipe them dry with kitchen paper and arrange on a work surface.

5. Apply the spice paste liberally to both sides of each piece of fish. Place a piece of fish on top of each banana leaf square and wrap up like a parcel, securing with bamboo skewers or string.

6. Place the parcels on a baking tray and bake in the preheated oven for 15–20 minutes, until cooked through. Transfer to plates and serve immediately.

BAKING, DESSERTS & DRINKS

Sweet and spicy flavours can complement each other
surprisingly well, as you'll discover with this irresistible
selection of spice-infused cakes, puddings and drinks.
Go ahead and indulge in smooth Chocolate Mousse
with a Chilli Kick; Spicy Squash Cake; Carrot, Fruit
& Cardamom Buns; or blast your socks off with
a Chilli & Wasabi Bloody Mary!

CHOCOLATE MOUSSE WITH A CHILLI KICK

| SERVES: 4 | PREP TIME: 20 mins, plus chilling | COOK TIME: 5 mins |

CHOCOLATE AND CHILLI MIGHT NOT FEEL LIKE A NATURAL PAIRING, BUT THEY WORK TOGETHER BEAUTIFULLY – A SUBTLE NOTE OF CHILLI BRINGS A DELIGHTFUL WARMTH TO THIS SMOOTH CHOCOLATE MOUSSE.

INGREDIENTS

150 g/5½ oz 70% plain chocolate, broken into pieces

pinch of salt

4 large eggs, separated

55 g/2 oz caster sugar

150 ml/5 fl oz double cream

1 tsp chipotle powder

2 tsp orange zest

100 g/3½ oz sour cherries

100 ml/3½ fl oz dark rum

55 g/2 oz roasted hazelnuts

1. Place the chocolate pieces in a large heatproof bowl set over a pan of gently simmering water and heat, stirring occasionally, until melted. Remove from the heat and set aside to cool.

2. Once the chocolate has cooled, beat in the salt, egg yolks and sugar.

3. In a separate bowl whisk the double cream until it has thickened slightly.

4. In a clean bowl whisk the egg whites until stiff peaks have formed.

5. Add the chipotle powder and 1 teaspoon of the orange zest to the chocolate mixture, then fold in the cream, followed by the egg whites. Divide between four glasses and place in the refrigerator for 2 hours to set.

6. Meanwhile, soak the sour cherries in the rum and roughly chop the hazelnuts.

7. Just before serving remove the mousse from the refrigerator and top with the rum-soaked sour cherries, the hazelnuts and the remaining orange zest.

CINNAMON-SPICED
SYLLABUB

| SERVES: 8 | PREP TIME: 10 mins, plus chilling | COOK TIME: none |

WONDERFULLY EASY TO MAKE, THESE LITTLE CLOUDS OF LIGHTLY WHIPPED CREAM LOOK BEAUTIFUL PILED INTO YOUR PRETTIEST GLASSES. YOUR GUESTS WILL LOVE THEIR MIDDLE-EASTERN SCENT OF CINNAMON AND ORANGE FLOWER WATER.

INGREDIENTS

juice of 2 lemons

½ tsp ground cinnamon, plus a pinch to decorate

1 tsp orange flower water

100 g/3½ oz caster sugar

600 ml/1 pint double cream

1 tbsp chopped pistachio nuts, to decorate

2 tbsp pomegranate seeds, to decorate

1. Put the lemon juice, cinnamon, orange flower water and sugar in a large bowl and whisk briefly to dissolve the sugar. Add the cream and lightly whisk until it just comes together as barely solid – this should take no more than 1 minute.

2. Spoon the syllabub into eight small 100 ml/3½ fl oz glasses. Sprinkle with the remaining cinnamon, the pistachio nuts and pomegranate seeds. Cover and chill in the refrigerator for at least 1 hour, or up to a day. Serve cold.

TIP

SYLLABUB SHOULD NOT BE THE TEXTURE OF TRIFLE TOPPING, SO BE CAREFUL NOT TO OVERWHISK IT AFTER ADDING THE CREAM.

APRICOTS POACHED IN ROSEWATER & CARDAMOM WITH GINGER YOGURT

| SERVES: 4 | PREP TIME: 20 mins | COOK TIME: 15 mins |

THIS IS ONE OF THE EASIEST DESSERTS TO MAKE, AND THE APRICOTS WILL BRING SOME SUNSHINE TO THE TABLE. YOUR GUESTS WILL BE DELIGHTED BY ITS EXOTIC FRAGRANCE AND GENTLY SPICED FLAVOUR.

INGREDIENTS

150 g/5½ oz caster sugar

6 green cardamom pods, lightly crushed

1 cinnamon stick

¼ tsp rosewater

350 ml/12 fl oz water

4 apricots, halved and stoned

1 tbsp dried edible rose petals, to decorate (optional)

GINGER YOGURT

100 g/3½ oz Greek-style natural yogurt

2.5 cm/1 inch piece of fresh ginger, peeled and finely grated

1. Put the sugar, cardamom, cinnamon, rosewater and water in a saucepan, stir and cook over a low heat until the sugar has dissolved.

2. Increase the heat to medium–high, bring to the boil, then lower in the apricots using a slotted spoon. Reduce the heat to low and simmer for 5 minutes. Turn off the heat and leave them in the syrup for 10 minutes.

3. Transfer the apricots to a serving bowl using the slotted spoon. When cool enough to handle, slip off and discard the skins.

4. For the ginger yogurt, put the yogurt in a small serving bowl, stir in the ginger, cover and set aside.

5. Return the syrup to the heat and boil until reduced by half. Pour the syrup over the apricots, then scatter over the dried rose petals, if using. Serve the apricots with the ginger yogurt. If not serving immediately, leave them to cool, then cover and chill in the refrigerator and serve cold.

TIP

ROSEWATER COMES IN DIFFERENT STRENGTHS, DEPENDING ON THE MAKE. ADJUST ACCORDING TO YOUR BRAND AND TASTE.

INDIAN
RICE DESSERT

| SERVES: 4 | PREP TIME: 20–25 mins, plus soaking and chilling | COOK TIME: 30–35 mins |

FOR THIS DISH, GROUND RICE IS COOKED IN THICKENED MILK WITH APRICOTS, RAISINS, ALMONDS AND PISTACHIO NUTS, WITH THE EXOTIC AROMA OF ROSEWATER AND CARDAMOM. IT IS BEST SERVED CHILLED.

INGREDIENTS

good pinch of saffron threads, pounded
2 tbsp hot milk
40 g/1½ oz ghee or unsalted butter
55 g/2 oz ground rice
25 g/1 oz flaked almonds
25 g/1 oz seedless raisins
600 ml/1 pint full fat milk
450 ml/15 fl oz evaporated milk
55 g/2 oz caster sugar
12 ready-to-eat dried apricots, sliced
1 tsp freshly ground cardamom seeds
½ tsp freshly grated nutmeg
2 tbsp rosewater

TO DECORATE

25 g/1 oz walnut pieces
15 g/½ oz shelled unsalted pistachio nuts

1. Place the pounded saffron in the hot milk and leave to soak until needed.

2. Reserve 2 teaspoons of the ghee and melt the remainder in a heavy-based saucepan over a low heat. Add the ground rice, almonds and raisins and cook, stirring, for 2 minutes. Add the full-fat milk, increase the heat to medium and cook, stirring, until it begins to bubble gently. Reduce the heat to low and cook, stirring frequently, for 10–12 minutes, to prevent the mixture from sticking to the bottom of the pan.

3. Add the evaporated milk, sugar and apricots, reserving a few slices to decorate. Cook, stirring, until the mixture thickens to the consistency of a pouring custard.

4. Add the cardamom, nutmeg and rosewater, stir to distribute well and remove from the heat. Leave to cool, then cover and chill in the refrigerator for at least 2 hours.

5. Melt the reserved ghee in a small saucepan over a low heat. Add the walnuts and cook, stirring, until they brown a little. Remove and drain on kitchen paper. Brown the pistachio nuts in the remaining ghee in the saucepan, remove and drain on kitchen paper. Leave the pistachio nuts to cool, then lightly crush.

6. Serve the dessert decorated with the fried nuts and the reserved apricot slices.

CHILLI & CHOCOLATE
CHURROS

| MAKES: 16 | PREP TIME: 35 mins, plus cooling | COOK TIME: 30–35 mins |

CHURROS ARE FRIED-DOUGH PASTRY SNACKS – IN THIS SCRUMMY VERSION, PLAIN CHOCOLATE, COCOA POWDER, CHILLI AND CREAM DO THEM PROUD.

INGREDIENTS

100 g/3½ oz unsalted butter, diced
225 ml/8 fl oz water
140 g/5 oz plain flour, sifted
large pinch of salt
2 large eggs, beaten
½ small red chilli, deseeded and very finely chopped
oil, for deep-frying
4 tbsp sugar
2 tsp cocoa powder, sifted

CHOCOLATE SAUCE

85 g/3 oz plain chocolate, broken into pieces
100 ml/3½ fl oz double cream
½ tsp vanilla extract
1 tsp dried chilli flakes, crushed

1. To make the chocolate sauce, put the chocolate and cream into a heatproof bowl set over a saucepan of gently simmering water and heat until the chocolate is melted. Remove from the heat and stir until smooth, then stir in the vanilla extract and chilli flakes. Set aside and keep warm.

2. Put the butter and water into a large saucepan over a low heat and heat until the butter has melted. Bring to the boil, remove from the heat and tip in the flour and salt. Beat thoroughly until the mixture is smooth and comes away from the side of the pan. Leave to cool for 5 minutes, then gradually beat in the eggs to make a thick and glossy paste. Beat in the chilli.

3. Heat enough oil for deep-frying in a large saucepan or deep-fryer to 180–190°C/350–375°F, or until a cube of bread browns in 30 seconds. Spoon the paste into a large piping bag fitted with a large star nozzle and pipe four 10-cm/4-inch lengths of the paste into the hot oil. Fry for 2–3 minutes, turning frequently, until crisp and golden. Remove with a slotted spoon and drain on kitchen paper. Keep warm while frying the remaining mixture.

4. Mix together the sugar and cocoa powder on a flat plate and toss the warm churros in the mixture to coat. Serve immediately with the chocolate sauce for dipping.

SPICES FROM BARKS, FLOWER BUDS & ROOTS

Spices can be sourced from arils, barks, dried flower buds, stigmas and roots, or from dried fruits or seeds. Here are a selection falling into the first category, as well as some mixed-spice combinations.

Cinnamon (see opposite, above left) is obtained from the inner bark of the *Cinnamomum* tree, which is native to Sri Lanka. The bark is dried and rolled up to make the long, slender tubes that characterize this spice. Cinnamon is also sold as a powder. Cinnamon is used in both savoury and sweet dishes.

Cloves (see opposite, bottom right) are the aromatic dried red flower buds of *Syzygium aromaticum*, an evergreen tree from eastern Indonesia. They have a hard surround and contain an oily compound that creates the distinctive warm, sweet, aromatic taste. Cloves are used to give aromatic qualities to hot drinks and are often used in spice blends.

Coriander also known as cilantro, is used for its leaves and seeds. The leaves have a subtle citrus quality whereas the dried coriander seeds, of which there are two in each fruit, have a much stronger lemony flavour and bring warm, spicy overtones. Ground coriander is used as a key feature of various spice mixtures, such as garam masala and harissa.

Curry powder is a premixed combination of spices, usually chilli powder, turmeric, coriander, cumin, ginger and pepper. Strengths can vary from mild to strong. It it believed to have been created by the British to recreate the depth of flavour in Indian spice dishes, although spice mixtures are also common throughout Asia.

Ginger is a hot, fragrant spice obtained from the rhizome of the Ginger plant *Zingiber officinale,* and the bulbous roots are widely used in southern Asian cuisines for drinks, soups, sauces and baking. It is available fresh or ground and can be used in sweet and savoury dishes.

Mace is obtained from the aril of the nutmeg plant, *Myristica fragrans* – the aril is the dried reddish covering of the nutmeg seed. The flavour, although similar to nutmeg, is lighter and sweeter and it has a more intense aroma.

Saffron is a spice from the flower stigma of the saffron crocus, *Crocus sativus* (see opposite, above right), which is native to south west Asia. The flowers each have three vivid crimson stigmas, and it is from these that the threads are collected and dried. It is available in bright-red threads, which carry a musty, floral aroma and flavour. Labour-intensive to produce, saffron is one of the more expensive spices.

Turmeric (see opposite, bottom left) comes from the root of *Curcuma longa* and has a peppery, bitter flavour with orange and ginger overtones. It is used in mustard, which gives it its bright-yellow shade.

Za'atar is the name of a herb, but also of a spice mixture made from a combination of dried herbs, spices and seeds such as sesame seeds, dried sumac and salt. Za'atar is widely used in Middle Eastern cooking.

SPICY
SQUASH CAKE

| SERVES: 8 | PREP TIME: 35–40 mins, plus soaking | COOK TIME: 1¼ hrs |

BUTTERNUT SQUASH ADDS A RICH TEXTURE AND DEPTH TO SWEET CAKES AND BEAUTIFULLY COMPLEMENTS DRIED FRUIT AND WARMING SPICES.

INGREDIENTS

50 g/1¾ oz sultanas

10 g/¼ oz unsalted butter, for greasing

450 g/1 lb butternut squash, peeled, deseeded and diced (prepared weight)

150 g/5½ oz unsalted butter

150 g/5½ oz caster sugar

50 g/1¾ oz almonds, chopped

50 g/1¾ oz Italian mixed peel

finely grated zest of 1 lemon

1½ tsp ground cinnamon

1½ tsp ground ginger

85 g/3 oz khorasan flour

1 heaped tsp baking powder

2 eggs, separated

10 g/¼ oz icing sugar, for dusting

1. Put the sultanas into a bowl, pour over boiling water to cover and leave to soak.

2. Preheat the oven to 180°C/350°F/Gas Mark 4. Grease and line a 23-cm/9-inch round springform cake tin.

3. Put the squash and butter into a saucepan. Cover and cook over a medium heat for about 15 minutes, until soft. Tip into a bowl and beat until smooth.

4. Stir in the sugar, almonds, mixed peel, lemon zest, cinnamon, ginger and drained sultanas, and mix well to combine.

5. Sift together the flour and baking powder, tipping in any bran remaining in the sieve. Gradually beat into the squash mixture.

6. Beat the egg yolks for about 3 minutes, until thick. Fold into the squash mixture.

7. Whisk the egg whites until they hold stiff peaks. Fold carefully into the mixture using a large metal spoon. Spoon the batter into the prepared tin.

8. Bake in the preheated oven for 1 hour, or until a skewer inserted into the centre comes out clean. Turn out onto a wire rack to cool. Dust with the icing sugar just before serving.

CARROT, FRUIT & CARDAMOM BUNS

| MAKES: 16 | PREP TIME: 50–55 mins, plus standing/rising | COOK TIME: 30–35 mins |

THE CARROT TAKES CENTRE STAGE IN THESE MOREISH SCANDINAVIAN-STYLE BUNS. BURSTING WITH GLACÉ FRUIT AND LIGHTLY SPICED WITH CARDAMOM, THEY ARE HEAVENLY WHEN EATEN FRESHLY BAKED.

INGREDIENTS

140 g/5 oz carrots, sliced
375 g/13 oz strong white flour, sifted
2 tbsp easy-blend dried yeast
3 tbsp golden caster sugar
2 tsp ground cardamom seeds (from about 24 pods)
½ tsp salt
125 g/4½ oz unsalted butter
1 egg, lightly beaten
5 tbsp lukewarm milk
10 g/¼ oz flour, for dusting
1 tbsp oil, for oiling
150 g/5½ oz chopped glacé fruit
1 egg yolk
1 tbsp cold milk
10 g/¼ oz icing sugar, for sprinkling

1. Put the carrots in the top of a steamer and steam for 15 minutes until tender, then purée in a blender until smooth. Set aside until needed.

2. Line a baking tray with a silicone sheet. Put the flour, yeast, caster sugar, cardamom and salt into a large bowl and mix to combine. Melt all but 2 tablespoons of the butter and leave to cool slightly. Mix the beaten egg with the lukewarm milk and the melted butter. Stir into the flour mixture, then add the carrot purée. Mix to a soft dough.

3. Turn out the dough onto a floured board and knead for 10–15 minutes until silky. Transfer to a lightly oiled bowl, cover with clingfilm and leave to stand in a warm place for 1½–2 hours, or until doubled in size. Turn out onto a floured board and knock back to get rid of the air. Roll out thinly to a 44 x 30-cm/17½ x 12-inch rectangle.

4. Melt the remaining butter and brush it over the dough surface. Scatter over the glacé fruit, taking it to the edge of the dough, breaking up any clumps.

5. Roll up the dough from the long edge into a log. Slice into 2.5-cm/1-inch rounds and place on the prepared baking tray. Cover with clingfilm and leave to stand for 30 minutes. Meanwhile, preheat the oven to 200°C/400°F/Gas Mark 6.

6. Mix the egg yolk with the cold milk and brush over the buns, then bake in the preheated oven for 10–15 minutes until golden.

7. Transfer to a wire rack to cool, then sprinkle with the icing sugar. The buns are best eaten freshly baked.

CHOCOLATE
PECAN BROWNIES WITH CHILLI

MAKES: 12	PREP TIME: 30 mins	COOK TIME: 20–25 mins

HOW ABOUT SOME GORGEOUSLY STICKY, CHEWY BROWNIES WITH A DIFFERENCE? THE CHILLI FLAVOURING IN THESE IS SUBTLE ENOUGH TO WAKE UP THE TASTE BUDS WITHOUT SHOCKING THE PALATE.

INGREDIENTS

50 g/1¾ oz unsalted butter, softened, plus extra for greasing

100 g/3½ oz unrefined cane sugar

3 eggs, beaten

100 g/3½ oz self-raising flour

75 g/2¾ oz cocoa powder

1 tsp dried chilli flakes

about 1 tbsp rum

100 g/3½ oz pecan nut halves

1. Preheat the oven to 180°C/350°F/Gas Mark 4. Grease a 20-cm/8-inch square or equivalent-sized rectangular shallow baking tin or tray.

2. Using a wooden spoon, beat the butter with sugar in a warmed bowl until pale and fluffy. Alternatively, process in a food processor. Beat in the eggs, a little at a time, adding a little flour if the mixture begins to curdle. Switching to a metal spoon, gently fold in the flour, cocoa powder and chilli flakes. Stir in the rum and add enough water until you have a cake mixture that drops easily from the spoon. Taste and see if you need to add a little more chilli. Fold in the pecan nuts, reserving a few of the best for the top.

3. Pour the cake mixture into the prepared tin, smoothing it into the corners. Sprinkle the top with the reserved pecan nuts.

4. Bake in the preheated oven for 20–25 minutes, or until crusted on top but still not quite set. Remove from the oven and cut into 12 squares while still warm.

SPICED PUMPKIN
TARTLETS

SERVES: 4	PREP TIME: 30 mins, plus cooling	COOK TIME: 40 mins

THESE LOVELY INDIVIDUAL TARTLETS HAVE ALL THE FLAVOUR OF TRADITIONAL LUSCIOUS PUMPKIN PIE. THEY'RE SIMPLY DELICIOUS SERVED WITH COFFEE, OR AS AN INDULGENT DESSERT, WITH LOTS OF WHIPPED CREAM OR VANILLA ICE CREAM.

INGREDIENTS

10 g/¼ oz butter, for greasing
400 g/14 oz peeled and deseeded pumpkin, cut into 1-cm/½-inch pieces
10 g/¼ oz butter
1 tbsp maple syrup
10 g/¼ oz stem ginger in syrup, finely chopped
¼ tsp cinnamon
¼ tsp allspice
135 g/4¾ oz filo pastry
2 tbsp rapeseed oil, for brushing
10 g/¼ oz icing sugar, for dusting

1. Preheat the oven to 190°C/375°F/Gas Mark 5. Lightly grease four 10-cm/4-inch tartlet tins.

2. Place the pumpkin on a baking sheet and dot with the butter. Roast in the preheated oven for 5 minutes, then stir and return to the oven for a further 20 minutes, or until the pumpkin is beginning to brown.

3. Stir the maple syrup, ginger, cinnamon and allspice into the pumpkin and cook for a further 5 minutes. Leave to cool.

4. Cut the pastry into twelve 10-cm/4-inch squares. Brush four of the squares with oil. Place a second sheet of pastry on top of each, at an angle to the first so that the points of the squares do not align – you are aiming to create a star shape. Brush with oil again and repeat with the remaining pastry sheets to make four stacks, each with three layers.

5. Transfer the pastry stacks into the prepared tins, press down gently, and bake in the preheated oven for 8–10 minutes, or until crisp and golden.

6. Fill the pastry cases with the pumpkin mixture. Dust the tartlets with the icing sugar and serve immediately.

CHILLI & AMARANTH
CORNBREAD

| **MAKES:** 1 loaf | **PREP TIME:** 20 mins | **COOK TIME:** 55 mins, plus cooling |

THE COMBINATION OF SWEETCORN AND CHILLI BRINGS A NEW DYNAMIC TO CORNBREAD. THIS CAN BE SERVED IN MANY WAYS, SUCH AS WITH STEWS AND CHILLIES, WITH DEEP-FRIED CHICKEN OR SIMPLY PAIRED WITH A FRESH SALAD.

INGREDIENTS

2–3 fresh red chillies, or to taste

90 g/3¼ oz amaranth flour

100 g/3½ oz white flour

115 g/4 oz coarse polenta (cornmeal)

1 tbsp baking powder

1 tsp bicarbonate of soda

1½ tsp salt

50 g/1¾ oz sugar

125 g/4½ oz Cheddar cheese, coarsely grated

3 eggs

225 ml/8 fl oz buttermilk

70 g/2½ oz butter, melted and cooled slightly, plus extra for greasing

60 g/2¼ oz fresh or frozen sweetcorn kernels, thawed if frozen

1. Preheat the oven to 200°C/400°F/Gas Mark 6. Preheat the grill. Grease a 900-g/2-lb loaf tin.

2. Place the chillies under the preheated grill and cook, turning occasionally, for 5–7 minutes, until blackened all over. Remove the skins and seeds and finely chop the flesh.

3. Sift together the amaranth flour, white flour mixture, polenta, baking powder, bicarbonate of soda and salt into a large bowl. Stir in the sugar and cheese.

4. Whisk the eggs with the buttermilk and melted butter until well blended.

5. Make a well in the centre of the flour mixture and pour in the egg mixture. Mix together with a fork, gradually drawing in the dry ingredients from the side.

6. Stir in the chillies and sweetcorn and spoon the batter into the prepared tin, levelling the surface. Bake in the preheated oven for 40–45 minutes, until a skewer inserted into the centre comes out clean.

7. Leave to cool in the tin for 10 minutes, then turn out onto a wire rack and leave to cool completely.

LIME & CHILLI
SORBET LOLLIES

| MAKES: 8 | PREP TIME: 15 mins, plus cooling and freezing | COOK TIME: 10 mins |

THESE PALE, CHILLI-SPECKLED SORBET STICKS ARE A TWIST ON THE CLASSIC LEMON SORBET, BUT HAVE A HIDDEN KICK FROM THE CHILLI. FOR A LESS SPICY VERSION, REDUCE THE AMOUNT OF CHILLI.

INGREDIENTS

100 g/3½ oz caster sugar

1 red chilli, deseeded and very finely chopped

400 ml/14 fl oz water

4 large limes

8 very thin slices from a small lime

1. Put the sugar, chilli and water in a saucepan. Place over a medium–low heat, stirring, for 6–8 minutes, or until the sugar has dissolved. Increase the heat to medium–high and bring the mixture to the boil, then remove from the heat.

2. Finely grate the zest of 2 of the limes into the mixture and stir. Cover and allow to cool completely; this will take about 1 hour.

3. Squeeze the juice from the 4 limes and stir it into the mixture.

4. Pour the mixture into 8 x 60 ml/2 fl oz ice-pop moulds and place a lime slice into each mould. Insert the ice-pop sticks and freeze for 5–6 hours, or until firm.

5. To unmould the ice pops, dip the frozen moulds into warm water for a few seconds and gently release the pops while holding the sticks.

CHILLI & WASABI
BLOODY MARY

| SERVES: 1 | PREP TIME: 20 mins | COOK TIME: none |

THIS ZINGY COCKTAIL OFFERS NO HALF MEASURES IN TERMS OF ITS HEAT. SAVOURY COCKTAILS ARE THE NEW TREND, AND THIS VERSION OF BLOODY MARY, WITH CHILLI POWDER, LIME JUICE, WASABI AND BULLDOG SAUCE, WILL HIT THE SPOT.

INGREDIENTS

1 measure vodka
1 measure sake
½ measure lime juice
½ tsp Korean chilli powder
¼ tsp garlic granules
2.5-cm/1-inch piece fresh ginger, grated
1 tsp fish sauce
½ tsp wasabi paste
2 tsp tonkatsu bulldog sauce or other hot sauce
whole ice cubes
175 ml/6 fl oz tomato juice
mooli radish stick, to decorate

1. Mix together the vodka, sake, lime juice, chilli powder, garlic granules, ginger, fish sauce, wasabi paste and bulldog sauce in a Collins or highball glass, using a bar spoon.

2. Stir well, making sure all the ingredients are well combined.

3. Add a few ice cubes and the tomato juice and stir again.

4. Decorate with the mooli radish and serve immediately.

TIP
THIS IS A DELIGHT WHEN SERVED WITH OYSTERS – AND YOU CAN ADJUST THE SEASONINGS TO TASTE!

VEGETABLE TUMMY TREAT

SERVES: 1	PREP TIME: 15 mins	COOK TIME: none

WAKE UP YOUR BODY AND STIMULATE YOUR DIGESTIVE SYSTEM WITH THIS FRESH-TASTING ORANGE-AND-TOMATO DRINK. THERE IS ALSO A KICK IN THE TAIL DELIVERED BY THE CHILLI TO SHAKE UP THOSE TASTE BUDS!

INGREDIENTS

3 oranges, zest and a little pith removed

1 carrot, halved

2 tomatoes, roughly chopped

125 ml/4 fl oz chilled water

1 small green chilli, halved

2 celery sticks, thickly sliced

2 tsp hemp seed oil

1. Cut 2 oranges in half and feed them and the carrot through a juicer. Pour the juice into a blender. Roughly chop and deseed the remaining orange, then put it, the tomatoes and water in the blender and whizz until smooth. Add the chilli and celery and whizz again until blended. Pour into a glass, stir in the hemp seed oil and serve.

INDEX